KV-433-418

THE POLITICAL CONUNDRUM

Wales and its Politics in
the century's last decade

WA 1143173 3

Series Editor: *MEIC STEPHENS*

The Political Conundrum

Wales and its Politics in the century's last decade

Clive Betts

**UNIVERSITY OF GLAMORGAN
LEARNING RESOURCES CENTRE**

Pontypridd, Mid Glamorgan, CF37 1DL
Telephone: Pontypridd (01443) 480480

Books are to be returned on or before the last date below

2 6 SEP 1997

9 NOV 1997

1 2 MAR 1998

1 0 JAN 2003

GOMER

1143173/3

First Impression — 1993

ISBN 1 85902 011 9

© Clive Betts

All rights reserved. No part of this book may be reproduced, stored in a retrieval system, or transmitted in any form or by any means, electronic, electrostatic, magnetic tape, mechanical, photocopying, recording or otherwise, without permission in writing from the publishers, Gomer Press, Llandysul, Dyfed, Wales.

Printed in Wales by
J. D. Lewis and Sons Ltd., Gomer Press, Llandysul, Dyfed

Learning Resources
Centre

The General Election of 1992 may have broken the Labour Party for ever. It went into the contest believing victory was there for the taking. Right up to the day before the poll, Wales too believed that a change of government was on the way. The shock of that early result from Basildon, which produced only a miniscule swing of 1.3% from Tory to Labour, reverberates still. Labour's fourth Election loss in succession was far more devastating than the number of seats won would suggest: the Party's gain of 42 seats was far less significant than its inability to manage a voting swing in Britain of more than 1.6%, and that in the depth of the United Kingdom's worst recession since the Second World War.

Since that fateful and surprising night, little of political significance has happened on the surface of Welsh politics. But hidden below the torpor which has afflicted Wales since the defeat of the Devolution referendum of 1979, and the later demise of the Social Democratic Party, are trends which seem to be leading up to one of those great political upsets which afflict a nation every seventy years or so.

In 1922, the political map was changed for the rest of the century when Ramsay Macdonald—a nationalist, although in the Lloyd George tradition—was returned as Labour member for Aberavon to become Leader of the Opposition. The significance was not so much that a Welsh seat was yet again playing host to one of the United Kingdom's foremost politicians; it was that Macdonald and his colleagues had broken (for ever?) the power of the Liberal Party in industrial Wales. At the previous Election in 1918, Wales had returned 21 Liberal and 10 Labour MPs; now the precise opposite had happened: 18 Labour men were returned, and only 12 Liberals of assorted types. Industrial Liberalism was decimated as young radical Labour tigers swept forward, leaving only one MP from the old Lib-Lab order still in place—the rather exceptional Sir Alfred Mond in Swansea West.

British politics may be heading once more for such an upset. It will not happen overnight—the 1922 revolution was twenty years in the making—and this time Wales will follow rather than lead. And the driving force may be regions rather than social class, regions within Wales as well as in England.

What has been happening on the ground in Wales has only been noted fitfully by newspapers and the broadcasting media; they must inevitably focus on the events of the previous day in order to catch and retain people's interest. We journalists are, in addition, often inhibited by the rules of our craft which demand that every word of a report is capable of justification, and that there must be a willingness to present both sides of an argument. In England, academics can fill a gap; in Wales, too few academics deal with present-day politics, and even then they are constrained by the need for fairness to all sides.

This essay is the fruit of quite a few years of quietly watching what is going on, and speaking to some of the main protagonists, whose off the record views are sometimes radically different from what they say for publication. To those ladies and gentlemen, my thanks. In some ways, the picture I paint here is radically different from received wisdom in Westminster. But that should be no surprise: MPs and the journalists who cover them—an in-bred system if there ever was one—are far too often woefully cut off from what is happening in the depths of the country which elects them. Whether the great political upset I have spoken of will in fact happen, only time will tell. The ingredients are there. But where is the spark?

The Conservative Party

One of the clichés of Welsh politics is that the Welsh Tories are an English gaggle, and that the strength of their support can be judged from the Census returns on the number of immigrants in any given locality. For the persistence of that myth, thanks are due today to Wales's leading political publicists—Plaid Cymru—and in the past to rural, Welsh-speaking writers and ministers who failed to come to terms with the inexorable growth of the English language—which they equated with Toyrism—in the more sophisticated market towns of the areas where they lived.

A study of the pattern of Conservative voting in the Wales of the past will reveal a very different basis for Toryism, and do much to explain the Party's support for the Welsh language. That is not to say, however, that Thatcher's minions are the natural party of the Welsh-speaking small farmer; far from it! But as that near-peasant form of economic activity is slowly outmoded, the Conservative Party can be expected to occupy a far more prominent place throughout Welsh rural constituencies.

The Tories' advance was greatly facilitated by a decision taken quietly about eight years ago. Under the rather uncommunicative Ted Thurgood, Central Office Agent for Wales, an Englishman married to a Welsh-speaker, the Party took a decision which, in time, should finally kill that canard. From the large, but rather dilapidated, suburban house in Whitchurch, Cardiff, which is the Tory HQ in Wales, went forth the edict that Wales must no longer be regarded as a training-ground in political manoeuvres for young English officer-types seeking a grander command elsewhere.

Some of these High Speed Train day-return specialists provided us with quite a bit of fun: there was, for instance, Den Dover, now MP for the safe seat of Chorley in Lancashire, who was master of the quick—and rather silly—phrase when he stood in Caerffili in 1974, of the 'Roll over with Dover' kind. Or James Arbuthnot, Captain of Fives at Eton, educated at Cambridge University, barrister, member of Kensington and Chelsea Royal Borough Council, who was drafted in on a short-term contract to fight Cynon Valley in 1983 and at the subsequent by-election. Thoughts of writing a send-up vanished at the sight of a candidate who related well to the working-class electorate and who was obviously enjoying himself, as he watched most of his vote vanish into the maws of SDP candidate Felix Aubel. The last laugh most emphatically went to Arbuthnot: he had noticed that Aubel possessed a couple of weaknesses—particularly for hanging. During the long hours as they watched Labour's votes being weighed, Arbuthnot discussed the political way of the world with Aubel. By the end of the evening, the SDP candidate was on his way to joining the Tory Party. He was eventually off-loaded by Central Office on to the unsuspecting Conservatives of the hapless and hopeless Caernarfon constituency at the same time as Arbuthnot took over Sir Winston Churchill's old seat of Wanstead and Woodford.

Despite the inability of Central Office to force constituencies to adopt favoured candidates—the knowledge or belief that Whitchurch or Smith Square is supporting a particular candidate is said to be a certain vote-loser—the news of the new preference has had a dramatic effect: not only are almost all candidates now Welsh, but in the Welsh-speaking constituencies they almost all speak the language. The same sea-change has come over Tory selection committees as affected Labour at almost the same time: no matter how good the outsider—and frequently with both parties exceptional English candidates applied—Labour constituencies now go overwhelmingly for Welshmen. With the Tories, the result in rural Wales was not always quality; but that is to miss the point. These candidates were standing in seats which are at present unwinnable; but they are respected local names and by their candidacy the Party was building itself a future locally.

The depth of Welsh support in the past for the Tories is usually under-estimated by their opponents. Over a century ago, the Conservatives gained between 44% and 51% of the vote in almost all the Welsh borough seats, whether Welsh or English-speaking. Even with David Lloyd George the eventual incumbent, Carnarvon District registered from 1885 to 1910 between 38% and 52% voting Conservative; as the boroughs included were, in the spellings of those days, Nevin, Pwllheli, Criccieth, Carnarvon, Conway and Bangor, with a proportion of English-only speakers in 1901 of under 16%, it can hardly be said that all those Tory voters were Englishmen. Indeed, the 1901 Census indicates that the constituency housed about only 1,300 men unable to speak Welsh—and not all would have possessed a vote—while at the election the previous year the Conservative candidate had won 2,100 votes.

Just across the water on Anglesey there has lurked for decades a substantial number of Tory voters. Keith Best's victory there in 1979 was no doubt assisted by English immigration, but it was also helped by characters such as Welsh-speaking journalist and political maverick John Eilian Jones who gained 35% of the vote in 1966, a short while before the island had started to become a retirement-home.

It may seem fanciful to go back a century for an explanation of current voting patterns, but the patterns set by the Victorians may still persist. Perhaps we can see an explanation for the high Tory vote on the island in the higher standard of farmland there, in the size of farms at the turn of the century, and in the high proportion at that time which were owned rather than rented by their occupants.

Interesting insights into the loss of Brecon and Radnor to the Tories in 1992 can also be gleaned from those faraway days. When the Liberals swept almost all before them at the end of the last century, it was Radnor in rural Wales for which they had to fight hardest. The reason seems to have been that it was a constituency where, although it housed few immigrants, the Welsh language was long dead. In neighbouring Brecon, the Welsh language was at that time still very much alive, and, although the farming was very similar, the Conservatives regarded the seat as such a lost cause that in 1900 they left it uncontested (although the presence of a southern industrial fringe, now removed, probably had an effect on their decision). During the 1992 Election, it was in Brecon that hill-farmers could say they thought Richard Livsey was the only candidate, while it was in Radnor that the Liberal Democrats admitted they were weaker. And could the strong working-class support for the Tories in parts of Cardiff today be due in origin to the religious arguments and vote-switching of 1885 by the Catholic working-class of Grangetown and South wards? Any observer can trot out dozens of reasons why the events of ninety years ago are irrelevant to voting today. But sometimes voting traditions can be passed on through generations to produce in neighbouring areas, apparently identical economically and socially, radically different voting patterns.

Despite the Tories' long history in winning Welsh votes, it is only recently that they have begun to feel at home when dealing with the Welsh language. The change seems to have come about in parallel with society's (including Welsh-speaking society's) changed attitude to the native tongue. Perhaps, indeed, the Tories have lagged—they certainly did not lead. But despite lagging, they have been able securely to take the lead over Labour.

The problem for Labour, of course, is that far too many remember George Thomas (now Viscount Tonypandy) as Secretary of State for Wales, and his blunt refusal to do almost anything until forced to it. We remember the car tax discs campaign and how 'impossible' it was to produce a bilingual version. In those days, the discs gave an abbreviated form in letters for the month of expiry; only when the Welsh Office was about to be made to look foolish through a mass campaign of refusing to display discs did Mr Thomas accept the display of the expiry date in the form of numerals, a method later taken up by the Department of Transport itself. Add that to the current problems over establishing more much-needed Welsh-medium schools in Labour-controlled West Glamorgan and the scene has been set for considerable suspicion about the Labour Party's intentions.

Yet the fact remains that Labour wins the support of most Welsh-speakers. According to the Beaufort Research Omnibus Survey, the Party is currently gaining 50% of that section of the electorate, compared with 25-30% for Plaid (presumably reflecting that Party's strength in the Welsh-speaking West and North), 20% for the Tories, and about 7% for the Liberal Democrats. How is it then that a Tory Party which attracts so much less support from the Welsh can be apparently so much more favourable to the language? The answer lies in that very failure to attract that support. Firstly, in the seats the Tories hold the language is usually not a major issue, either because the constituencies are highly anglicized, or because they are rural. The language conflict, where it occurs—leaving aside the tiny but vociferous Education First group in Carmarthenshire—has been so often a phenomenon found in industrial districts, yet another aspect of the generations-old fight to preserve jobs for the those who hold them already and to prevent another, 'outside', group from muscling in.

The Conservatives can therefore afford to be generous to the language. Viewed simplistically, they have less to lose in terms of votes. They are also more willing to view the language issue in cultural rather than jobs terms. While there are plenty of Colonel Blimps (Rtd) within the Tory ranks, there are also far more culture-vultures than can be found in a Labour Party ward meeting. It is surely not insignificant that John Major and Dafydd Wigley can get on so well together (they are still paired for voting purposes in Parliament) when both their wives are keenly interested in music, Norma an opera-buff and Elinor a harpist. So many times lately have language-enthusiasts expressed their thankfulness that they are dealing with a Conservative rather than a Labour Government. Although Labour can be as good or better than the Tories—the Labour Party contains many sincere friends of the language—there exists a deep fear of the prejudice lurking in ward branches. Not that the Conservatives have no prejudices dogging some of their meetings. This prejudice usually appears in the guise of the Thatcherite opposition to barriers to economic and industrial efficiency, which are the very reasons, of course, why the language was allowed to decline so rapidly by its speakers a century ago. The main spokesman for this view currently is the Confederation of British Industry—while a more favourable attitude is taken by the Institute of Directors, the same people but with different leaders. But it is to the CBI that Tory Ministers must genuflect, and genuflect Sir Wyn Roberts did during his press conference in December 1992 introducing the Welsh Language Bill. Despite a clause which can easily be read as subjecting privatised utilities to the Bill's demands, Sir Wyn, in response to a question, read a prepared answer of which —according to someone who was watching his face—he did not believe a word: 'We have taken the view that the public utilities are very much in the private sector and we are anxious not to do anything which will impede the development of the private sector and the Welsh economy generally. We do not want to lay burdens on the private sector that they would not bear elsewhere in the UK.' Beautifully Thatcherite, from one of the least Thatcherite of Government ministers, but enough to keep the CBI and the back-woodsmen happy. When the Bill is passed, it will be what its clauses say which will be crucial, not comments by a Minister in a press conference.

Is it too difficult to see the Tories being able to make direct electoral use of their language policies? The Party is within an ace of taking back Ynys Môn, a 3.3% swing would give them Ceredigion and Pembroke North, they are the challengers in Meirionnydd Nant Conwy (although a very long way behind, and hampered by little organization in the constituency), and in 1987 they were runners-up to Labour in Carmarthen, only 8% behind, with Rod Richards, now MP for Clwyd North West, as candidate (although they slumped badly in 1992 with a local, but non-Welsh-speaking farmer as candidate).

The Conservatives have always argued that eventually Wales will come their way. They have spoken of a country that is changing, becoming more prosperous, of the disappearance of the collectivist impulse that has driven the industrial Valleys for decades. For so many years this seemed like whistling in the wind. Yet, as I write, some of these things are beginning to happen. The golden M4 Corridor has crossed the Severn, Clwyd is experiencing an economic renewal with the building of the A55 (although too much of it is dependent on English commuting), Welsh unemployment is now almost identical with that of Britain and South-East England (although the problems which remain are far deeper than those of the South-East); and while the collectivist impulse is still thriving in the Valleys, the counter-culture of go-getting small businessmen is at last taking root in a country which for so long regarded initiative as possibly a trifle sinful. This gradual re-creation of Wales in a Tory image presents their Whitchurch office with an opportunity, and their opponents with a dual challenge: first, to acknowledge what is happening, and secondly, to adapt in order to meet the challenge to their existing policies and attitudes.

The Tory base vote is far larger and more faithful than revealed by the Party's see-sawing number of MPs in Wales. Between Thatcher's dream of a rugger-team from her Welsh benches (14 Tories were returned in 1983) and the disaster of 1966 (only three MPs returned) there lay a difference of only 2.7 in the percentage of the Welsh vote that the Party won, a rise from 28.3% in 1966 to 31%. Indeed, the most remarkable fact of post-war Welsh politics has been the stability of the Tory vote. Excluding 1945, when they left nine seats uncontested (usually giving Liberals a free run) and the disaster of October 1974, their vote has varied little, between 27% and 32%, while Labour's has see-sawed between 61% and 38%, and Plaid's between 11.5% and 7.3% in the period since 1970, when the Nationalists first fought every seat.

Tory support has been concentrated naturally enough in middle-class and in English-speaking rural Wales. The 1922 Election, the second after the abolition of the Tory-inclined boroughs, was not untypical: Tory seats were confined entirely to suburban Cardiff and Newport, and Monmouth. Eventually, parts of the present county of Clwyd were added. Just this sort of voting pattern helped to perpetuate the propaganda view of Tories as being English (or so anglicized that they may as well have been). Since the Second World War, the Party's history has gone through three stages which bid fair eventually to cause a major upset in Welsh politics. The first lasted until 1964: it consisted of anti-Socialist deals with the Liberals who until then had held most of the seats in Welsh-speaking Wales; the effect of having a live-in Tory lover lingers almost thirty years later in the sheer conservatism (and unionism?) of rural Liberal associations. The Montgomery Association was first reported to have queried the existence of a Welsh Liberal Party in 1962, and at the Party's 1992 Autumn Conference they and Conwy were reported as having failed to pay their dues to the Welsh party, thereby imperilling the Welsh Party's exhibition and publicity stands at both the National Eisteddfod and the federal Party Conference, as well as County Council Elections funding and six other budget-lines listed in the Annual Report.

The Parties' votes over the years

	Lab	Con	Lib	Plaid	Govt
1992	50	29	12	8.8	Con
1987	45	30	18	7.3	Con
1983	38	31	23	7.8	Con
1979	47	32	11	8.1	Con
10.74	49	24	16	10.7	Lab
2.74	47	26	16	10.8	Lab
1970	52	28	7	11.5	Con
1966	61	28	6	4.3	Lab
1964	58	29	7	4.8	Lab
1959	57	33	5	5.2	Con
1955	58	30	7	3	Con
1951	61	31	8	1	Con
1950	58	27	13	1	Lab
1945	59	24	15	1	Lab

Percentage of the vote gained by each Party at consecutive General Elections, and the name of the Party which formed the Government.

The Conservatives did not fight all seats in Wales until 1964, Plaid not until 1970, and the Liberals not until October 1974, while one Labour MP was returned unopposed in 1945.

The second stage saw the Tories fighting on every front, and quite a mess they made of it through much of Welsh-speaking Wales. Apart from the two constituencies, both only partly Welsh-speaking, which they had held almost continuously since the war (Conwy and Denbigh), their performance until 1979 was abysmal. In three seats (Carmarthen, Cardigan and Merioneth), a contest could mean a lost deposit. Only in Caernarfon and Anglesey were decent results obtained, and they weren't much to write to Smith Square about. Over these five Elections, the average Tory vote in the Welsh-speaking seats was: Carmarthen, 10%; Cardigan, 16%; Caernarfon, 19%; Merioneth, 12%; and Anglesey, 28%.

The 1979 Election brought both a Thatcherite revolution and a surge in Tory support throughout the Welsh areas which has been maintained ever since. From propping up the polls, the Conservatives are now the main challengers almost everywhere. That 1979 success has shot them on to a higher plateau from which they cannot be shifted. Their average polls in the four Tory-won Elections has become: Carmarthen, 26%; Ceredigion and Pembroke North, 28%; Caernarfon, 20% (has the presence of Dafydd Wigley as MP hindered their growth here?); Meirionnydd Nant Conwy, 27%; and Ynys Môn, 37%. With such results, is it any surprise that successive Secretaries of State, abetted without a doubt by Minister-for-life Sir Wyn Roberts, discern considerable voting-value in boosting the Welsh language?

While it is no doubt satisfying for the Tories to be able, with the aid of English immigrants, to enjoy a knees-depth paddle in the sea of Welsh-speakers, the Whitchurch office bemoans their near-complete failure to make inroads into a far more substantial battery of Welsh seats. These are the 16 constituencies in the Valleys, solidly held by Labour since 1922 when the workers' revolution finally put paid to the Liberal ascendancy in Wales. Every decade or so, Whitchurch decides to see whether Labour locally possess any wish to follow their southern-English colleagues into near-oblivion. Pressure is put on local constituencies to capitalize on their General Election votes by fielding candidates for Town and County Hall. But nothing much happens; 'I'm sure we'll win the Valleys,' a Central Office official told me, 'but it won't be in my time.' James Arbuthnot persuaded the Cynon Valley Tories to capitalize on the 1984 by-election, but their challenge soon faded out in the face of poor votes. Even youngish, enthusiastic Valley-born locals were unable to break the deep anti-Tory traditions of communities which remember Winston Churchill as the Home Secretary who in 1910 ordered troops into Tonypandy to maintain order in the face of a strike by 30,000 miners. Almost all the mines have now gone, miners total barely 300, and yet enough of the dust of the coal-seams lies on the consciousness of Valleys voters to prevent them supporting Churchill's Party at local elections.

Only in Ogwr have the Tories made a mark. In an area which Plaid Cymru used fondly to imagine would eventually be theirs—although they had not much more than Councillor Ted Merriman to show for their advance—the Conservatives have now taken over as official opposition to Labour. It is a presence, though, that is largely restricted to the coastal zone—Bridgend, Porthcawl and some of the villages and estates around. This is almost an extension of the Newport-Cardiff-Vale of Glamorgan voting belt. But while those three areas have relied to some extent on English middle-class immigration, it seems to be the upwardly-mobile Valleys Welsh who are the meat of the Tory invasion here, even if one of their leaders is a lively Englishman, David Unwin. Perhaps Valleys-Welshness can be discerned in the plotting and desperate infighting which saw Peter Hubbard-Miles first replacing an outsider-Englishman as Parliamentary candidate—through the use of almost every trick which a Valleys Labour Party could dream up, plus a couple extra—then winning the seat, losing it, splitting the local constituency over council issues, and finally losing even his local authority seats, although he regained his county seat at the final county elections of 1993.

Some Labour Party members see the quintessence of their own Party in the Valleys as the existence or imagined existence of complex plots swirling around every smoke-filled meeting. If there is any truth in this, the Tory Party has clearly arrived in Ogwr! Perhaps the Tories have won a break-through in coastal Ogwr because this is an area which gives the voters no physical reminders of the Valleys of their parents. With the vanishing of the geological barriers has disappeared the blockages in the brain.

Yet there exist serious weaknesses in the Tory position in Wales, principally in local government. The Thatcherite revolution that did so much to pep up the Party in the rest of Britain, particularly in southern England, has had no effect in Wales. The number of Tory councillors seems to have peaked in 1976 at 209. In the *annus mirabilis* of 1979, it fell to 194, and has kept slipping since, to only 129 at the last count. Significantly, the Party has failed badly to make much impact in elections to the three Councils where they were once so powerful—Newport, Cardiff and South Glamorgan. Perhaps the Party lacks the local government characters of the past, such as Sir Charles Hallinan and others. Perhaps Labour's local government people have so thoroughly seized the middle ground in Wales—although not in many other regions of Britain—that they have left no political room for the Conservatives.

If Welsh Tories show at times so little ability to adapt to competition, it is perhaps sad that they are likely to be about to be presented with two new Welsh Parliamentary seats as the result of the boundary changes. With Pembroke and Carmarthen the largest electorates in Wales, and both growing rapidly, a new seat is bound to be created in Dyfed. The logical division will be along Milford Haven, thus neatly splitting between two constituencies the industrial Labour voters of the former dockyard towns which have made Pembroke Labour on several occasions. Another seat is due in Clwyd, although its location is less clear.

The Liberal Democrat Party

The 1992 Election was an unmitigated disaster for the Liberal Democrats. The grouping which managed second place in 18 seats in 1983—even in Aberavon with such an uninspiring candidate as flower-farmer Sheila Cutts—lost two of its three constituencies, leaving barrister Alex Carlile stranded as Leader of a Party of One. With few outside the Party believing that Geraint Howells's old Ceredigion and Pembroke North constituency could be regained, and the Party itself apparently afflicted with a death-wish, it seemed time to pen the obituary for the Party in the region which had kept the Liberal flag flying for decades during which it had come close to lacking even a flag-post in England.

Yet death does not seem to be closing in yet. A major effort is under way to re-align the party from a past which has vanished to enable it to take advantage of a future which is already appearing in England, and which should soon be appearing on the Welsh horizon.

The Party whose significant Welsh presence in Parliament had been for so long from Welsh-speaking Wales is apparently deciding that that area is now beyond its grasp. In 1945, the Liberals held Anglesey, Merioneth, Cardigan and Carmarthen, (Caernarfon had just been lost), plus Pembroke, Montgomery and University of Wales; at the time, Wales provided more than half the strength of the Parliamentary Party. The new scheme is that the Liberal Democrats should become the Party of Anglo-Wales. A commission has been established to attempt to map a new way forward. Although the commission's initial public moves seemed more directed to policy, possibly as the result of a misunderstood mandate, its underlying aim is likely to be far more fundamental. In any case, it will be good to hear new thoughts on policies, which seem likely no longer to be the dirty subject it appeared in Wales in the aftermath of the take-over of the Social Democratic Party.

Perhaps most important, now that it has left behind the need to attract Nationalist votes to ensure Geraint Howells's survival, the creation of clearer differentiation between the Liberal Democrats and Plaid Cymru is being attempted. That differentiation rests on the use of the words 'Offa's Dyke', beyond which Plaid are said to be of no significance—in distinction, of course, to the importance of the Liberal Democrats on both sides of that boundary! Perhaps, of course, Mr Carlile realizes more than most (he is Welsh-born of Polish-Jewish extraction) that Eastern Europe faces decades of upheavals that will blacken the names of some nationalisms, and may not exactly do too much good to Plaid's hopes of expansion.

The arrival of a new leader represents the breath of hope from that 1992 electoral disaster. While Richard Livsey was Alex Carlile's predecessor, the ghost that seemed to rule in the background was that of Geraint Howells. Some people found it difficult at times to distinguish Geraint's policies—which were frequently drawn up

17

with little regard for conference decisions—from those of Plaid Cymru. Nationalists quietly claimed him as almost one of them. On Welsh-medium schools, for instance, he stood solidly behind the Plaid view, which was not quite that of his own Party. For a Welsh Assembly he was a most enthusiastic advocate. His support for the rural Welshness of language and community was much purer than that of many in Plaid—who, being middle-class, cared more for town and college than for village and farmyard.

Yet Geraint was not a good Party leader; his politics were those of that of the glad-hand and the presence, of being seen in the right place at the right time, whether Eisteddfod or funeral. Richard Livsey was impelled into the job in the hope he would prove better as a national leader. He was better, but only to some extent. After having farmed for some years near Cross Inn, Llanon in the heart of rural Cardiganshire, he was too much tied to the Howells school of policy.

Carlile hails from another policy school, which has in the past been dubious about the advantages of a Welsh Assembly (although, as Leader, he refuses nowadays to brook any questioning of past failure to adhere to this policy), and which has been much keener about keeping an eye on England. He also hails from the school of politics which rejects the old-fashioned, rural view, still favoured in Ceredigion, that politics is only for election-time. David Owen, when leader of the SDP, reckoned that this rural lethargy was a severe hindrance. Because he had to fight to unseat the Tory Delwyn Williams, Carlile realizes the dangers of a moribund Party (for such it was when Montgomery was bequeathed to him). He also appears to possess the political sharpness, plus the quickness, brightness and breadth of interest and vision, to set a revival in action. He commands, seemingly, the ability to delegate, for with a thriving court practice he is not around as often as some of his political colleagues would wish him to be. His is the background most suitable for the Party's current re-alignment: Welsh, but not strongly so; a rural seat, to keep the yokel-members happy; a practice in England to emphasize cross-border links; and a willingness to learn enough Welsh to meet the demands of end-twentieth century Wales and of the Welsh-speaking districts.

The Welsh Liberals are badly in need of success; not only have

18

they for years been performing worse in Parliamentary elections than their English colleagues, but they are also being worsted in Town and County Halls. While the English have continued to advance in local elections, the Welsh Liberals have slowly but steadily been overhauled by Plaid Cymru. After the 1991 district elections, the Liberal Democrats were able to boast only 101 councillors, compared with Plaid's 136. The drive had vanished from the heart of their local election effort: while Plaid was slowly advancing, councillor by councillor, into new territory, the Liberal Democrats were left largely relying on the districts where their strength went back some years—Cardiff, Swansea, Colwyn and Aberconwy—while their generally non-political rural representation slowly ebbed away.

The 1993 county result saw hints of a revival, although the party was still lagging behind Plaid, with 34 seats to the Nationalists' 41. Yet, although the Lib Dems gained 12 seats (in every county bar Mid Glamorgan), Plaid managed an advance of 14 (in every county bar South and West Glamorgan). And the advance paled in contrast to the revolution in England, where the party gained 380 seats (producing a total of 839), compared with Labour's gain of only 104 (giving a total of 1,118).

The contrast with what has been happening to Liberal Democrats in southern England could not be starker. While rural Wales was once the Liberal heartland, that role is now being taken by the swathe of constituencies stretching from Land's End to almost the River Test in Hampshire, plus a string of south-eastern coastal towns. In 27 consecutive constituencies—only a few seats, mainly urban, are excluded—the Liberal Democrats are the main challengers to the Tories, and have been slowly but consistently increasing their lead over Labour for twenty years, often leaving that Party by today with so few votes that they would have lost their election deposit under the old rules. The result has been the ringing of alarm bells in Conservative Central Office as it realized that the Liberal Democrats are building up the sort of regional base they have lacked since the Wales of the 1950s. This time the swathe of constituencies lies not amidst swirling Celtic mists but in the rich farming and outer-commuter belts of the South, once secure Tory territory. And the number of seats involved is far higher, too. The first stage of that advance was to kill off Labour; the second is to win over the more radically minded Tories. Despite the last Election being a poor one for the Liberal Democrats, these were seats where their vote continued to grow; in only one did it fall more than the national average. A private report for the Tories commented, 'This is acutely dangerous. The threat to Conservative hegemony in the South of England is very real indeed.' The researcher blamed his own party's 'ineffectual districts' and lack of organization for council elections. Had the researcher taken a longer historical perspective he might have espied in operation the more fundamental sociological change which so terrified the Labour Party; while Labour can perhaps write off these southern shires, can they take such a benign attitude if the changing political perspective starts moving northwards, eroding first marginal Labour seats—as happened when the SDP was active —and then the heartlands?

The county and Newbury by-elections on the same day in May sparked off a war of press releases between Labour and the Liberal Democrats about who had won. While Labour had returned the largest number of councillors—becoming the largest party in former Tory strongholds such as Suffolk—their number of gains in such areas was tiny. Instead, the Tory vote split: former Tories swung overwhelmingly to the Liberal Democrats, perhaps enabling that party to break out of its ever-expanding ghetto of South-Central and South-West England. Conservatives dismiss these advances as typical mid-term blues; their significance may rather lie in the continuation and extension of that Liberal Democrat ghetto, which is moving, with each election, closer to becoming a series of strongholds for the successors of Lloyd George.

These southern electors seem to have taken a step which a host of opinion polls indicate the vitally-important socio-economic group C in Greater London may also be considering: these once-Labour voters are refusing to switch back to Labour after their flirtation with the Tories because of their former party's 'outdated' philosophy and policies. So far, their movement to the Liberal Democrats in Labour areas of Greater London has been limited to Simon Hughes in Bermondsey, and control of Tower Hamlets Council, although the old SDP also managed to win and hold the neighbouring riverside constituencies of Greenwich and Woolwich. Fears that the

Liberal Democrats could be about to make further advances help to explain the *Southern Discomfort* pamphlet from Labour's Giles Radice, who hails from England's south Wales, the Durham coalfield.

How much happier the Liberal Democrats are. As well as their growing strength in the South, they are also a Party to be reckoned with in diametrically-opposed parts of the kingdom. In the Highlands of Scotland and rural Wales their success seems based on the remoteness of those constituencies, on the belief among peripheral-region electorates that they are more likely to be served well by a candidate from a minor Party than by one who will become lobby-fodder for the Government or Her Majesty's Opposition. And in the South they can portray themselves as the radical successors to Labour.

The nearest of these successful southern seats to Wales is Hereford, which borders on Brecon and Radnor. The Hereford seat seems well enough organized to be winnable by the Liberal Democrats at the next Election; in early 1992, for instance, it registered the British party's third-largest membership gain, an increase of 133, on a total which was admittedly not revealed. But such hopes can scarcely be realistically held for Ceredigion and Pembroke North. A senior Party official told me, 'Plaid Cymru did not win that seat; we lost it. They did the work; we didn't.' It is claimed that the seat could be won back by hard (and dirty?) campaigning. But in being told that, I can hear between the lines—the locals are unlikely to want to get involved. They are too old, the numbers of activists are too few, there is no tradition of electioneering between elections, and (worst of all, because it betrays the weakness of the local Party) the number of councillors elected in 1991 was halved (from 16 to eight, most of them becoming Independents once more). Not that having Liberal Democrat councillors in Ceredigion has done much for the political profile as they scarcely ever met or acted as a group, and would have been horrified at any suggestion that a Whip should be appointed to ensure their support for agreed policies. Even Plaid Cymru has found it hard to politicize Ceredigion; Plaid's great success locally has been through their links with urban English immigrants. These people believe politics is about policies. Being newcomers, they have had no time for or understanding of what used to make local politics tick, which was the politics of connection, neighbourliness and acquaintance. In that sort of world, MPs expected they would serve constituents rather than Party. In any case, the Liberal Democrat Party does not at present in Ceredigion engage in the lively politicking needed to attract the constituency back to the party fold, and neither is it likely to in the future, now that the lively local radicals are comfortably ensconced within Plaid Cymru.

The political tide has irrevocably gone out for the Liberal Democrats in the Welsh-speaking West. It went out in Caernarfon and Merioneth at the first hint of a realistic challenge from the Welsh Nationalists. The Anglesey vote, which had hung on at a respectable level for some years after the loss of the seat in 1951, plummeted when John Lasarus Williams broke through for Plaid in 1970; the slide in Merioneth really got under way that same year when Dafydd Wigley doubled the Plaid vote there; while the several stages of the descent of the Liberal vote in Carmarthen to silly figures seem linked to Plaid intervention. The two Parties, with quite similar policies, plainly cannot co-exist, and it is the Liberals, weighed down with age and seriously lacking the vigour of youth, who have had to give way. In the two partly-Welsh speaking seats where the Liberals have continued to make a showing—Denbigh and Conwy—it is Plaid which has had to move over and prop up the poll. In this pair of constituencies, the proportion of Welsh-speakers is not sufficiently high for the electorate to believe that Plaid's appeal possesses any hope of success.

Yet the fading of the Liberals from much of rural Wales has been slow compared with their eviction from the industrial South. In 1900 they were supreme throughout almost all that area; in 1918, they still held seven purely industrial seats; after the 1922 Election, they retained only one; and within ten years the Party had faded almost completely from the scene. Making a come-back appears impossible. For the Liberal Democrats, these are some of their weakest seats in Britain. Where 'Liberals' have held council seats, the gentlemen concerned have not infrequently been found not to be Party members. Organization has been non-existent: of the 14 Welsh constituencies with too few members a couple of years ago to form a constituency Party, most were in the Valleys. All too often, several of the Valley constituencies have acquired a candidate only weeks before a General Election as some valiant outsider has been drafted in to fly the flag.

To some extent, this failure has been a reflection of the political conservatism of the Welsh Party. The urban, street-level radicalism which reformed the Party in the rest of Britain from the 1960s onwards has been largely absent in Wales. The beards-and-sandals brigade never reached a Welsh Liberal conference; frequently, few people wearing any kind of footwear reached the conference room: seldom are the numbers present large enough to justify a proper hall, and the 1986 conference came close to being abandoned because so few delegates were left, and those who remained were so bored. The tiny knot of radicals from Swansea and Cardiff managed to gain only a little influence; on occasion they seem to have been deliberately frozen out from political influence.

From the point of view of the Valleys, the radicalism of the early years of the century has totally departed from the Welsh party. Perhaps this has been because of the dead hand of the countryside, where for much of the first half of the century the Conservatives stood down in rural seat after seat to give the Liberals a free run in order to keep Labour at bay. Deals continued as late as 1959 in a varying mixture of Montgomery, Cardigan, Merioneth and Carmarthen constituencies. Despite the attempts by such as Montgomery MP and Party Leader Clement Davies in the early post-war years to maintain some hint of a leftward stance, the rural Party has often been strongly anti-Labour. In the case of Cardigan and Carmarthen, it was the dual fear of the Socialism of the Valleys and of corporate trade unionism which are so much at odds with the individualism found in a farming community. In addition, com-munities which never united on party lines retained a deep dislike of the Labour Party machine. Propping up the Labour Government until 1979 was undoubtably a major factor in the surprise defeat of Emlyn Hooson in Montgomery, although as important were his poor constituency organization and a hyper-active Tory candidate backed by a rejuvenated local Party.

The formation of the Social Democratic Party out of the then near-ruins of Labour should have been the remedy for an ailing Welsh Liberal Party. Here was a Party whose leading members included politicians whom Labour-voters could trust. Members talked knowledgeably about both industrial problems and trade unions. For the few years of the SDP's existence, Welsh politics were immeasurably enlivened. Characters such as Gwynoro Jones, Peter Sain Ley Berry, Tom Ellis, Clive Lindley and Tony Jeremy proved that Welsh-based political thought can exist outside Plaid Cymru. The SDP's host of carefully-researched (in comparison with other parties) policy documents brought a new radicalism to centre-Party politics in Wales and, I am authoritatively told, a few concerns to old Liberal hands who had spent too long keeping the constituency Tories happy. For a time, despite the complaints of SDP leader David (now Lord) Owen, Welshmen and women were in the policy vanguard of a British political Party.

Dead that Party is, but yearnings for what it might have been continue. Alex Bird, in the Cardiff Trades Council magazine *Union Eyes*, commented on the 1992 General Election result, 'The centre tendencies of the Tory and Liberal camps could in time coalesce into a new SDP-type grouping, who knows?' And Charles Kennedy, Liberal Democrat (and former SDP) MP for Ross, Cromarty and Skye, mused around the same time, 'What we need is a viable alternative to the Tories which is basically what the SDP tried to be. That is a Party which embraces the free market with enough intervention as is necessary to protect and promote the interests of the poor, and which is not class-based in its approach.' For some reason, neither of these commentators believes that the present Liberal Democrats are the Party to break through into Labour territory (although they have managed it occasionally). It is surely significant that the Party's current strength in Cardiff tends to be in the areas where the Tories are or were a political power.

The failure of the SDP to carve out a strong-enough niche to resist a merger with the Liberals is not my story, but the effect in Wales certainly comes within my compass. In England, the Liberal Party split over the merger, with a splinter-group going off to its own oblivion. In Wales, the Liberals simply took over, giving in the first joint elections senior positions to previous-unknowns who had never set foot in the powerful Alliance Committee which had supervised the in-step march of the two independent parties, the Liberals and the SDP. According to Gwynoro Jones, David Owen had warned that a merged Party would end up like the old Liberal Party—half dead on its feet in Wales. And that is precisely what happened. The SDP newcomers—who were sixty per cent Tory—faded away. The conference in 1988, at which the leadership of the merged Party was voted in, saw an attendance of only eighty, compared with 240 when the SDP alone had conferred. The Liberal Democrats' voting would have done the TUC proud: in vote after vote, Liberals beat SDP members by almost exactly the same margin. Top of the poll for the executive was the previously unkown John Annetts, of Brecon and Radnor. Old SDP hands allege a whipped and pre-arranged card-vote was organized by three named Liberals who had never taken a prominent (or indeed any) part in the Alliance Committee. And when the Executive chose the new Party's officers, a similar carve-up seemed to have happened; elected Secretary was the previously (and since, to the press) unknown David McBride, of Brecon and Radnor. That Election sparked the combative Gwynoro Jones, of Swansea, former Alliance Committee chairman who had been a candidate for the chairmanship of the new Party (he was beaten by Cardiff Liberal councillor Jenny Randerson, at that time new to Welsh national politics), to comment after the meeting, 'We were trying to create a position of influence. But because of the machinations of the old Liberals, we have landed up with a raw recruit.' It has not been like this in England, I am told. Is it because of this Liberal *coup d'état* that most SDP members have faded away? At the end of 1992, the Welsh Party's executive committee of 34 included only five from the SDP, and one of them was stepping down. SDP members could hardly have felt comfortable in the Welsh Liberal Democratic Party, as formed.

Since its formation, repeated questions have been raised about the Welshness of the merged Party. The SDP and the Alliance Committee (which in Wales linked that party to the Liberals) never had any such problems because of their determination to forge a path for England to follow. However, the Welsh Liberal Democrats, being the Liberals writ slightly larger, suffer sometimes from an identity crisis: are they really Welsh, or are they the subsidiary Welsh branch of a British Party, a Lloyd George Remembrance Society, or perhaps a moderate version of the Welsh Nationalist Party? Or perhaps they are no more than a collection of *Focus*—

publishers, trawling the streets for the latest minor complaint that the other parties have missed?

Their Welshness could certainly sometimes be questioned. It was not only that in 1967, on the formation of the Welsh Liberal Party, one of the most powerful constituency parties—Montgomery—asked what was going on. As late as 1992, the Welsh Party conference was told that that same constituency was refusing to pay dues, thus jeopardising a series of national (Welsh) initiatives and plans. How important, indeed, to Liberal Democracy is the Welsh Party? Not very, it would seem. So much of the real work is nowadays done at federal (British) level that it was proposed in 1992 that formal Welsh (and Scottish) representation on the Federal Policy Committe be abolished.

And then there is the argument over whether the existence of the nation of Wales is really relevant to an individual mid-Wales constituency Party. The battle has been fought recently on the grounds of cash. The Party, unlike other political parties, has for years pursued an ultra-conservative financial policy, apparently ensuring that every penny is in the bank before a single penny is spent. Arguments from Party activists that the Party must spend first in order to profit later from increased membership have fallen on deaf ears.

The most recent example of the folly that such an attitude can engender was the future of the headquarters office in Cardiff, an episode which also raises the question of what Wales means to some Welsh party members. Short of cash as usual, the Party decided some months before the 1992 Election that their newly-occupied office, which replaced ancient premises elsewhere in the city centre, would be closed in the December after the poll, when the short-term lease ran out. In true parsimonious Cardi spirit, the Executive decided that the national HQ should share premises with a mid-Wales constituency office. A fair amount of anti-Cardiff feeling was also involved, with mid-Wales members jealous of the use which city councillors and branches could make of it, and the special attention they imagined they could receive from their own neighbourhood office. This feeling welled up at the Party's autumn conference in Swansea, where General Election campaign supremo and City Council Liberal Democrat leader Mike German failed to be re-elected to a full seat on the Party's executive, having to make do with a one-year casual vacancy. Perhaps, too, Mr German had upset too many rural backwoodsmen with his blunt demands for some political action.

It seems to be a sign of the more outward-looking attitude of the Welsh Party's new Leader that this was one of the decisions which failed to survive the General Election defeats. Alex Carlile considered a move to the heartlands as a retreat to 'obscurity', and he personally helped financially to guarantee the new five-year lease.

The role of Welshness in the new Party continues to be a problem. What is the basis on which the Liberal Democrats win seats? On their liberal philosophy, on their Welshness, or on their *Focus* magazines, with items such as: 'Coun . . . recently found the pillar box on the corner of . . . and . . . full to the brim. He has written to the Post Office Users' Council as this is not the first time this has happened. We will report the results in due course.'

It sometimes seems as if ensuring the local letter-box is emptied is a substitute for political philosophy. Perhaps indeed the Liberal Democrats are right in assuming that local politics are really more about the local voter than about high politics, about good government rather than treating the Council chamber as a mini-House of Commons. As government gets bigger, perhaps the role will increase, too, for the Party which puts the little man first, rather than the views and prejudices of Walworth Road or Smith Square.

The Labour Party

On the day before the General Election of 1992, the Welsh Labour Party was *en fête*. As befits a party about to go into Government, Welsh organizer Anita Gale hired a suite at the Holiday Inn in Cardiff for a late-morning party. She was not so foolish as to call it a victory celebration—it was officially a thank-you to the press for their services during the campaign—but a celebration it swiftly became. The large suite was full of politicians, press people, food and drink. The press had turned up to see what the new Welsh Office and other Government Departments would look and work like, and the politicans to try out the Ministerial garments they fondly assumed they would be wearing later in the week. Speeches were given which assumed—credibly for the first time—that Neil Kinnock was on his way to Number 10, and that Barry Jones might be taking over Cathays Park. Former *South Wales Echo* journalist Alun Michael, caught by an awkward question, slipped naturally into the answer-dodging formula which has to be second nature to Government ministers. Only a worn-out John Smith, the Vale of Glamorgan candidate, looked dubious about the outcome of the following day as he related how he had spent most of his campaign canvassing in the extensive and usually Tory-voting Vale parts of the constituency he had won at the by-election of 1989.

Labour was not the only party exuding confidence that Wednesday morning; the Liberal Democrats in their suite of offices above a bookie's shop in St Mary Street hosted an up-beat breakfast-with-prizes party for the press. In their minds there was no doubt that tactical voting was going to do them well, perhaps even giving them the balance of power.

That Basildon result very early on Friday morning contradicted the television exit polls and halted both Parties in their tracks. Basildon was no freak: as the night wore on, it became clear that the South-East of England continued to be marked out so often as a no-go area for Labour. Advances were made, but nowhere near enough to see Kinnock in at Number 10. Indeed, the high number of seats won from the Conservatives turned out to be no guide to the poverty of Labour's British result. The Tories held on to an overall majority of 21 seats; this would have been their expectation on a votes lead of only 4%; in fact, they ended up 7.5% ahead (which should have given them 20 more seats than they secured), compared with 11.5% in 1987. This was the fourth successive Election when Labour had been trailing by 7% or more. As so many pundits had been suggesting, that 1987 gap was just too large to bridge. That Labour did deceptively well was because they had achieved a higher swing in marginal seats, partly because so many Liberal Democrats switched to backing the strongest anti-Tory candidate. Allied to that was a population drift which saw Labour seats getting smaller, and suburban Tory constituencies larger. Clearly, what had worked in favour of Labour in 1992 is unlikely to work next time around after the Boundary Commissioners have finished their work. Significantly, of the 13 seats Labour gained in the London area, 11 had electorates below the Boundary Commission's quota, sometimes seriously so.

Yet Labour's poor showing, in particular the way they have been ruthlessly sidelined yet again over almost all southern England, hardly applies to Wales, particularly the industrial South; any worries about the small increase in votes in Mid Glamorgan were swamped by the size of the majorities, while the Party's middle-class thinking members in South Glamorgan were (as in parts of Clwyd) rewarded with substantial advances. Admittedly, results in rural Wales were bad (except for Monmouth and Pembroke), but such areas have long been largely written off by outsiders, if not by party-optimists. As long as the industrial South and parts of Clwyd remain solid, Welsh Labour is happy. And, with the demise of the SDP challenge, and the failure of Plaid Cymru to make both marked and consistent advances (Gwent results were abysmal), there is clearly nothing to worry Labour's mandarins in the Valleys.

The local councils' battlefield

Percentage of political councillors elected, by party

	1973 CC	1973 DC	1976 DC	1977 CC	1979 DC	1981 CC	1983 DC	1985 CC	1987 DC	1989 CC	1991 DC	1993 CC
LAB	72	75	54	51	67	71	65	73	64	76	68	72
CON	18	15	26	37	21	18	21	13	17	10	13	8
PLAID	5	5	15	10	7	6	7	5	9	7	12	11
LIB	5	4	4	3	5	4	7	10	10	7	8	9

Due to rounding, totals do not necessarily come to 100.

Percentage of independent councillors elected

33	39	46	34	40	28	36	27	35	26	33	25

Few Independent and Others councillors were Labour; generally, their support and that of their voters would go at a General Election to Liberal, Conservative and Plaid, in that order.
CC: County council election. DC: District council election.

Increasingly, Labour is being seen as a collection of geographically -remote regional parties: industrial south Wales, inner London, central Scotland, the industrial towns of northern England. How much do they have to say to one another? There is vituperation, certainly, between inner London and the rest, plus a deep lack of understanding of why so much emphasis has to be given in London to issues of gender and orientation. Also there is dislike of the London Labour Party's leftward slant, of its concentration on Marxism and more new-fangled theories at the expense of service to its electors, and its predilection for confrontation with the Government, rather than accommodation, which is the Welsh way. Welsh councillors complain that London's local government has been of no help to the Party nationally. South Wales Labour MPs sometimes comment bitterly about 'arrogant' council leaders who have done 'no favours' for the rest of the Party.

The Labour Party in the Welsh Valleys clearly stands solidly on the traditionalist wing, which is hardly surprising considering the age of many of its members. While the typical English activist is by now middle-class, reading *The Guardian* rather than looking at *The Sun*, efforts by their equivalents to make a mark in industrial south Wales have been largely rebuffed. Labour in the Valleys still consists of the working-class, and therein lies the Party's tremendous strength. Together with central Scotland, this is the last area where the concentration of Labour-held constituencies is so dense that the socialist new-thinkers of the middle-class, with their frequent emphasis on ideology, can make no headway. When they arrive with their new ideas, they are likely to be given short shrift. The Party in the Valleys still retains that unbroken link with its solidly working-class, trades union predecessors of the nineteenth century. While Labour front-bencher Michael Meacher can refer to Party branches as being 'husks', and a journalist says they remind him of Potemkin Villages—facades hastily erected to keep the Tsar happy—such charges cannot easily be hurled at Valley branches, although membership totals have dwindled severely.

The split between working-class and middle-class in the Party is fundamental to its future, or lack of it. The leaders of the councillors' groups which control authority after authority in the Valleys are men (seldom women) of solid working-class credentials. To some of their MP colleagues, they are a joke, but they have still to be collaborated with—because of the power they wield—and they are even granted a grudging respect. An influential section of the Welsh Party believes that all would be well, and Kinnock would have been happily installed in Number 10, if only the British Party had consisted predominantly of men of their ilk. In fact, Labour's front bench is overwhelmingly dominated by university graduates, with a fair sprinkling of doctorates among them; room is found for only two men with a 'working-class' background, Tom Clarke, who proceeded as far as high school—although it is a moot point how many Party members would admit an 'administrator' who used to be Assistant Director of the Scottish Film Council to the working-class—and former-merchant navy steward John Prescott who was educated in a secondary modern school. Prescott is highly praised by some Welsh Labour members for his instinctive knowledge of and close contact with the working-class—he speaks what they think, it is said.

It is difficult for these sincere critics of the make-up of the modern Labour Party to realise that Prescott is probably the last of a long line. When Kinnock spoke in Cardiff of his pride at being the first member of his family to attend university, he was speaking also for many MPs occupying the front bench with him. Kinnock, for instance, talks of the regret he has felt sometimes for not having worked down the pit. He and his colleagues are often the first generation to have escaped a life of hard, manual work. Free education for all in the post-war world has ensured that working-class sons and daughters now possess a ladder by which they can climb out of their parents' class. Not all take it. But the Labour Party choses as its Parliamentary candidates men and women who have shown the willingness to make the most of the opportunities open to them.

Thus, bitter criticism of Labour Leader John Smith for his lack of links with the working-class is in truth a criticsm of progress itself. It amounts to a call for the clock to be put back. Yet gone for ever are the days when a Labour Cabinet could include four miners, a shop assistant, and a farm labourer who went to work at the age of 10; every one of those men would today be boasting degrees. Whether they would have maintained the close Valleys-type contact with the working-class voters who are the fount of Labour's power and strength is more doubtful. Many middle-class Labour MPs can certainly manage a measure of contact. But Party members would ask how they can possess the sort of deep knowledge of working-class problems and of poverty which can only come from experience. In other words, the Party's Parliamentary representation is drifting rapidly away from its electorate. The Party itself is being split between middle-class leaders and working-class followers. As the division widens, the danger increases of, on the one hand, the middle-class wandering off at a policy tangent because of their lack of personal experiences of the problems they are seeking to solve, and on the other of the workers deciding that Labour's leadership is no longer representing their true interests and wishes. Which is precisely what is happening.

The other danger which has beset Labour—mass infiltration by the hard left—has largely been avoided in Wales. Only in Swansea, Newport and Cardiff did there exist ward branches and constituency parties so weak as to be amenable to infiltration by the Militant bed-sit brigades of the early-1980s. Very few Militants penetrated to the Valleys—not because of the shortage of bed-sit accommodation, but because branches were too large and too unforgiving of entryism, whether Militant or middle-class. While Militant talk of Swansea's becoming another Liverpool—where the city council was dominated by members of that Trotskyist faction—was never fulfilled, the Party had a narrower escape locally than was ever admitted.

The Party in the Valleys is in some ways a social organization, representing almost the entire community. Labour's deep strength in the Valleys can be likened to that of Plaid Cymru in Gwynedd (or, as a Plaid member said of his own party, the Communist Party in the old Soviet Union): each Welsh Party possesses a symbiotic relationship with the community, the one because of class, and the other because of language. Labour's history, allied to the history of the Valleys themselves, has combined to ensure that the Party's greatest opponents, the Conservatives, hardly ever dare poke their heads above the parapet. Indeed, for years, Plaid also felt it was safer to keep a low profile in some districts.

The enduring strength of this working-class Labour Party, and its ability to lead Wales from even a minority position, has been seen in the proceedings of the Council of Welsh Districts, a body far more politicized (by Labour) than its equivalent, the Assembly of Welsh Counties. Labour's CWD politicking in the late-1980s ensured that there was little love lost between them and their opponents. In

1990, Labour lost control of Taff-Ely borough and hence of the CWD. But loss of voting control has not necessarily meant loss of political control. The tight political organization of the Labour group—meetings are on occasion attended by both Anita Gale and research officer Andrew Bold from HQ in Transport House—has enabled the party not infrequently to propose political initiatives which are gladly accepted by the non-Labour chair. Labour frequently second motions proposed by the controlling Coalition group, and then go on to give the only major speech on the issue. As a senior official said, 'Labour lost the majority, but nothing changed.' Labour's high profile is helped by some of the strong personalities on their side, especially Harry Jones, of Newport, their leader. So different is the Coalition's willing acceptance on occasion of Labour leadership, compared with Labour's condescending attitude to the opposition when they were in control. But then the Coalition suffers from its difficulty in taking a strong stance on some issues because of the diverse political views of its members, and the reluctance of many from rural districts to bring politics into local government. Indeed, it is becoming noticeable how often the start of CWD meetings is delayed because the Labour Group are still debating (or arguing?) long after the Coalition group has completed its preview of the agenda.

Also greatly changed is Labour's own attitude to losing power. At first, no doubt deeply shocked, they took an unpleasant, confrontational line. It took several months for wiser counsels to prevail, for the Party to accept that the line of co-operation with the Coalition Group which they have taken (bar a few histrionics for publicity or electoral purposes) is more fruitful.

Playing politics is, of course, what Labour local government in the Valleys is all about. And the Party is extremely successful at it, even if a whiff of Tammany Hall is produced. Occasionally, there has been the smell of corruption, seen at its worst in Swansea and the old Glamorgan. Fortunately for the Party, nothing occurred on the scale of the Poulson scandals in the north-east of England, which did so much—combined with the factional and fratricidal politicking of so many left-wing groups within the Party—to soil the perception of Labour as a party of idealism and welfare, and replace it with the image of a party of free-spending, public waste and corruption.

The contrast between south Wales and the ideologically-based constituency parties that exist in boroughs such as Brent could not be greater. In Brent, the middle-class organized Party is ideas-led. Some of those ideas are so unpopular outside the local caucus that they have threatened to wreck the Party nationally—and it is no use blaming papers like *The Sun* for the publicity it has given those excesses, because that paper does little more than accurately reflect the prejudices of so many Labour voters.

But at least Brent is not brain-dead. Attempts, however, to introduce new ideas into meetings of Valleys Labour council groups usually fall on exceedingly stony ground. Where are Labour's ideas for decentralization, passing power to tenants, pledging minimum service standards? Apparently not often considered by Welsh Labour groups. The group is not a place for ideas, I am told, but a place where councillors win pledges for their own wards, and where factions advance their territories. The group works within a system in which the councillor, rather than the paid officer, likes to consider himself supreme, on the minor problem as well as on major policy, a system in which the first point of contact for the voter should be the councillor's home rather than the Town Hall, Yet even internal Party critics admire the system. 'With their nepotism and paternalism, they are perhaps better politicians than me,' I was told by a leading Welsh national Labour figure. 'After all, it gathers in the votes.'

Yet this sort of party is restricted to the Valleys. Outside the industrial areas and the major towns, the Party is little more than the 'husk' which front-bencher Michael Meacher says it so often has become. The inability over some years to find anyone to stand for election for certain regional seats on the Welsh Executive seems to indicate that some rural constituencies have gone far in decline. Shades, surely, of the decline of the Liberal Party in Wales. It is difficult to imagine nowadays that Caernarfon and Merioneth were once Labour constituencies; now support at general election is down to 16% and 19%. Transport House is eager for the outside world not to write off the Party outside the industrial South. And indeed recent years have seen a reversal of past decline, with local election successes in Clwyd (the County Council is now marginally Labour-controlled, for the first time ever), and a smaller number in

Gwynedd. Yet these are small-town and council estate, not country-side, advances, and the Party advanced less than average throughout most of Dyfed, Gwynedd and Powys in the 1992 General Election.

What is the long-term future of Labour in the Valleys? What is to stop it stumbling down the path created by many once-strong constituencies in the south of England, where electoral support has halved, sometimes almost to vanishing point, at general elections in the last fifteen years? Sociologically, the Valleys have changed immensely over that period. The sociological base which they were given at their creation in the last century—homes within walking distance of a single work-place—has vanished. It was that base which allowed the close identity of Trade Union and Party, both fighting towards the same end. The single work-place (usually a pit) has long gone, as have some of the long-resident families. But most of the voters have remained and adapted. It is this adaptation which is worrying Marxist-inclined politicians—although not, if we are to believe it, the Labour Party itself.

In place of the old working-class a New Working Class has appeared, we are told. This is a yuppie working-class, consisting mainly of the children of miners. These off-spring are better educated, have often gone into white-collar jobs which are perhaps situated on the coastal belt to which they commute by car. If their job is still blue-collar, it could well be in a small factory with either no or weak union organization—certainly, the old solidarity of colliery lodge or large shop floor is absent.

And from this change in working conditions and background develops a change in politics as the old certainties and needs vanish. The main proponent of this view in Wales is David Adamson, of the University of Glamorgan. He reckons that it was the first stage in this sociological change which produced Plaid Cymru's advances in the Valleys in the 1960s and 1970s. A later stage, he argues, will see a Conservative advance—which has, of course, already happened in coastal Ogwr.

Yet whatever happens in the rest of Britain, it is dangerous to be too deterministic about the Valleys. Labour has had much experience of fighting back. Twenty years ago, the Party was under severe attack from Ratepayers in Ebbw Vale, Swansea and Port Talbot because of its lethargy. Where are the Ratepayers now? Plaid Cymru won and kept control of Rhymney Valley and Merthyr districts until 1979; where are Plaid's current councillors in Merthyr and in the mid and upper Rhymney Valley? And Cynon Valley's Parliamentary seat was due to be won by Plaid in 1974, we were told. Then, in 1983, the Social Democrat and Liberal Alliance swept forward to second place in all 12 Valley constituencies; where are their successors, the Liberal Democrats, now?

The truth is that Labour in the Valleys has shown an enviable ability to renew itself, usually (admittedly) on the basis of more of the same. Perhaps the efforts of Peter Hain in Neath herald a more basic change. Like Alun Michael (Cardiff South and Penarth), Hain hails from the Liberal tradition, which reveres the individual, while Labour (and indeed, Plaid Cymru) usually gives its support to the group. While Labour in the Valleys can be caricatured as holding out an open hand to the Treasury in London for financial assistance for its strongholds, the Liberal tradition would be more concerned with elevating the individual and maximising his potential. And that was the message which came out of Peter Hain's 1992 'New Agenda for the Valleys' conference in 1992, an event which doubly trod on traditional Labour toes—by ignoring existing frameworks and the 'good work' which they had done, and by inviting members of another Party onto a Labour platform.

One of the messages from that conference was that Valleys people have to stand more on their own feet, making greater use of their own abilities. This is an individualistic message of bettering oneself; its absence from Party policy has been clearly spelt out by Party modernizers (although not by the traditionalists) as a prime reason for the Party's dismal failure almost everywhere to realize that the working-class are upgrading themselves. It is argued that Labour's entire philosophy is now out-dated, being tied far too much to collectivism and to the declining trade unions, being far too concerned with representing deprived minorities, and failing to realize that the vast majority, working-class and otherwise, are doing quite well, thank you. We are here into the internal argument of Mods versus Ancients; to Labour's shame, it is an argument which is too little heard in Wales, a country where the Party has been far too complacent, too willing to refer to those far-off days of the 1966 Election when they took every seat bar three.

But it would be unfair to claim that the Welsh Party is totally unchanging. One of the biggest switches was the appointment of Caerffili MP Ron Davies as Shadow Welsh Secretary—in place of long-serving Barry Jones, Alyn and Deeside—with controversialist Rhodri Morgan, Cardiff West, and local government expert Paul Murphy, Torfaen, as his aides. At last journalists would be able to deal on Welsh matters with a first-rate Labour team possessing the knowledge, ability and confidence to speak out without delay when necessary.

Another big change has been in the attitude over the last decade towards the Welsh language. Hostility has generally concentrated at the grass-roots, which presumably explains the praise from Lord Cledwyn, former Labour MP for Anglesey, for the House of Lords as a superior debating chamber for language issues. It lacks the 'constituency influences' of the Lower House: 'The pressures are absent,' he said. By now, the antipathies of Labour's last period in government have largely vanished, with the departure of George Thomas to pastures new, and the general sea-change in attitude throughout the community. There is nothing to fault about the attitudes held by Rhodri Morgan (son of a Professor of Welsh), Alun Michael and Paul Flynn (all Welsh-speakers), while Shadow Welsh Secretary Ron Davies sends his daughter to a Welsh-medium school.

Yet worries persist. There is the attitude of West Glamorgan County Council with their failure to meet demand from parents for places in Welsh-medium schools. Perhaps this is the so-standard dislike for a language which you or your parents chose to forget. The Party's grass-roots do not seem in this county to be the sole cause of the problem; in addition, the local Party bigwigs and senior education officials bolster one another's hostility. In Mid Glamorgan, the competition with Plaid Cymru has gone out of the issue—for some years, Labour linked the language quite naturally with their electoral enemies Plaid Cymru, and were therefore unwilling to concede on the language issue. The point of change can be best marked by the visit of the National Eisteddfod to Rhymney, when the opposition to use of Welsh on road-signs suddenly evaporated within the county Labour group, the people ultimately with the power to pronounce whether or not such signs should be erected beside the highway. Yet, with reason, language enthusiasts are frequently dubious about the depth of the conversion-experience. The opposition lives on but—in the words of a senior local offical—those members are 'too lethargic' to match the energies of the pro-Welsh.

Not since *The Miners' Next Step* and similar revolutionary documents of the 1920s has Labour in Wales worn a red shirt. Today, in the councils it controls, it is essentially collaborationist with Government policies. Over recent years when English authorities have regularly had their budgets capped for a mixture of over-spending and extremism, Wales has escaped. What significance is there that the only Welsh council to have its spending capped this year was Aberconwy? Although Labour is a minority on that council, the party ignores Transport House guidelines and supplies most of the chairmen. A moderate Labour Party in the Council chambers has been faced by a moderate regime in the Welsh Office. Each suited the other; the butties born to rule in Wales facing the chappies born to rule from England; the right-wing Socialists faced the left-wing Tories. Was it any surprise that they have got on so well?

And so it was, until the Labour-led Assembly of Welsh Counties showed their frustration at 14 years of Tory rule by declaring that it was Labour who called the shots in Wales, not whatever Tory happened to occupy Number 10 or Cathays Park/Gwydir House. The issue was local government reform and how to strike back at the Welsh Office after the counties had maintained for too long that the only answer to Government plans for their abolition was that the eight should be transformed into giant unitary authorities. For long, the pugnacious, but humorous Graham Powell, Labour leader of Gwent, strove hard, in vain, to convert the AWC to a rejectionist line. Success came only when Russell Goodway took over the leadership in South Glamorgan and added his voice.

At that point, the group took leave of its moderate past, declared all-out war and used their majority to persuade the AWC to follow. Co-operation with the Welsh Office was refused over the vital talks which would lead to the mergers with the districts. Backing came from the trade unions, particularly NUPE, led by the Derbyshire firebrand Derek Gregory, who seems more politician than trades unionist.

As I write, a coalition with hard-left connotations seems in control, intent on ignoring British constitutional conventions. It is almost as if the Red Borough of Camden had transformed itself into the Red Republic of Wales. Watching these antics from the sidelines are bemused local authority staff (who seem to have been deprived of the assistance of their union NALGO in beating the best deal possible out of the Government) and several county chief executives —who had long realised that there is no way that a string of pressure-groups with conflicting demands, aided by the Wales TUC (to Tories, a voice of little significance), could defeat a Government possessing the majority to carry out a General Election mandate.

David Hunt, with his one-nation Toryism and open-door policy to (almost) anyone, was a good foil to the one-nation Labourism that had for so long been the like emanating from the party of the workers in Wales. Hunt was willing to listen, and sometimes to change. Welsh Labour MPs—led by the increasingly statesmanlike Shadow Secretary Ron Davies—refused to accept the non-co-operation line adopted by the 1993 Welsh party conference; they instead resolved to make use of that open door to try and argue 'sense' into the reforms.

How John Redwood, David Hunt's Thatcherite successor, will react to this intriguing split in the Labour Party cannot yet be foretold. A full-scale battle between the far-Left and the far-Right would be won by the latter, and do untold harm to Labour itself, because most of Wales will not tolerate such antics. But, unfortunately for those political vultures waiting for Labour to turn itself into a corpse, neither side is likely to provide Armageddon on this issue.

Plaid Cymru

The history of Plaid Cymru is the Welsh political success story of the second half of the twentieth century. It was the only party to make successful and enduring use of the youth revolt of the 1960s and the associated questioning of Establishment orthodoxy, which converted the then middle-aged Party from a minor pressure-group into a secure political party important enough to have on occasion to elevate expediency above principle.

Yet success through the 1970s, 1980s, and early-1990s will not necessarily be continued into the new century. For Plaid is stuck on a plateau, with few signs of its being able to climb from being a successful regional pressure group into a viable national Party. By region I mean, of course, that of the Welsh-speakers, and by nation I mean Wales. Plaid Cymru has made effective use of its formidable publicity machine to deny that it is stuck, and confined within the *Fro Gymraeg* (Welsh-speaking areas); post-General Election by-election successes have been supposed to presage a break-through into the populous and politically-critical southern Valleys. But, before considering that, let us examine what happened in April 1992.

In only five seats did Plaid's vote rise above 30% of the poll, and four of them were won by the Nationalists: Caernarfon (59%), Meirion-nydd Nant Conwy (44%), Ynys Môn (37%), Carmarthen (32%, where the Plaid candidate was a close second to Labour), and Ceredigion and Pembroke North (31%, a Plaid gain from the Liberal Democrats). The next seat was political aeons away: Llanelli, where Plaid polled just 16% and were pipped by the Tories. Plaid will, of course, protest that Marc Phillips, their able Llanelli candidate, occupies almost exactly the same position as did Cynog Dafis, the Ceredigion victor, in 1987, even to the extent of his votes being on a rapidly-rising curve (Marc Phillips's vote rose 50% from 1987 to 1992, while Cynog Dafis's rose only 26% between 1983 and 1987).

Yet although there are similarities between Ceredigion and Llanelli, the differences are greater. In the latter, the Welsh language is retreating from much of the constituency, although valiant efforts are being made by *Menter Cwm Gwendraeth*, the locally-based language movement, to revive it in the rest. One has to ask what is the attitude towards Welsh from those families, particularly in Llanelli town, which have willingly abandoned its use; how many are showing the antagonism towards Welsh so often seen in Swansea and parts of West Glamorgan, another area which has turned its back on the ancestral language?

Of greater significance is the state of the incumbent political party and its representative. No one could accuse Gareth Wardell, the energetic and incisive chairman of the Welsh Affairs Select Committee, of being ready for retirement or of lacking interest in politics. And whatever might be said of the constituency Labour Party, it is in far better condition than the Ceredigion Liberal Democrats have been for many a year. The ability to withstand a strong assault from Militant (which was a mixture of respected local figures and draftees from their Swansea West stronghold) could well illustrate a Party which has been strengthened and revived by conflict. In other words, although Plaid may be able to grow further, it will not be able to take advantage of the internal collapse of its main opponent, despite the sniping that continues still between Labour's left and right-wings.

That Llanelli's Labour Party has severe internal troubles is not doubted. How else could that party be losing so many local council seats to an incredibly odd mix of Liberal Democrats, Plaid, Greens, and even a Conservative (at the May 1993 county elections). What is notable is not the troubles, but the inability of any single party to capitalise on them. Each party won where the others were weak. Lib Dem gains, for instance, were in an area where Plaid has scarcely any representation. As has happened so often to Welsh Labour, their council vote has been imperilled, but not their Parliamentary support.

The Plaid political map is therefore currently largely the map of the country's Welsh-speaking areas; it is more precisely the map of those constituencies where Welsh is the habitual language and which lack a large English-speaking incisor. Where such an incisor exists, it is often of immigrants (frequently of many years' standing), and Plaid Cymru will usually have failed to make inroads into it. A party which is seen by the local electorate to be irrelevant to part of the constituency is thus incapable of winning the whole, and thus polls poorly in areas which would, in different circumstances, be part of its heartland. It is thus impossible to imagine Plaid ever being able to win in areas such as Conwy (where the Liberal Democrats have seized the baton because of the presence of English-speaking Llandudno), Clwyd South West, and Llanelli (although Plaid's Valleys campaign may have an effect there).

Beyond Llanelli, Plaid's General Election vote enters silly-territory, where a contest equalled a lost deposit—until the threshold was reduced to 5%. Yet there exists a group of six seats (including Llanelli) which could come right if Plaid were able to re-orientate itself. Three showed healthy—around 50%—increases in the vote in 1992: Cynon Valley, where the Party won 11% of the vote in 1992, and two of its Mid Glamorgan three gains in the 1993 county election; and Neath (11.3%) and Pontypridd (9.1%, although both latter results followed Parliamentary by-elections which had enlivened the Party locally). Highly significantly, the performance in both Cynon and Pontypridd occurred on the back of a healthy representation on the local councils. Lesser vote increases were registered in Rhondda (11.8%, up 2.9%) and Caerffili (9.7%, up 1.6%; the Party is strong on the local council). The last seat in this block—Clwyd South West—is radically different; this is a Welsh-speaking territory where advance is blocked by English-speakers. Perhaps that accounts for Plaid's poor performance there at the General Election (9.8%, up 1.3%).

Three seats comprise the next block in terms of General Election votes. The highest vote in this group was at Conwy, which is a seat bracketed linguistically, of course, with Clwyd South West. Performance in 1992 was poor: the vote fell by 0.5%. The other two seats are notable only in that they escape the truly-silly group of constituencies: they are Ogmore (6.3%) and Merthyr and Rhymney (6.1%).

Of the 22 seats remaining, there is little to say. These are the seats where Plaid tried hard to rope the Greens in on the basis that the votes of two parties' supporters should make some difference to the figures, and that it would be nice for someone else to help with the slog of fighting a constituency. On both accounts, the Green link seems not to have worked, as the votes remained miniscule and few Green supporters turned out. Deposits were lost, of course, in all 22 seats.

Yet it is these Valleys that Plaid President Dafydd Wigley regards as crucial to the future success of his Party. He can see as well as anyone the danger of Plaid Cymru becoming purely a language-Party; this does not mean Plaid would be home for all Welsh-speakers' votes. According to Colin Williams in *National Separatism* (1982), only 17.5% of Welsh-speakers voted Plaid in the mid-1970s; since then the figure has risen to 25-30%—but that rise is no more than in line with the increasing concentration of Plaid's votes in the

Welsh-speaking areas. In 1974, 35% of Plaid's vote was concentrated in Anglesey, Caernarfon, Merioneth, Cardigan and Carmarthen; in 1979, that figure increased to 43%, and last year it reached 54%. What that increasing concentration does mean is that Plaid Cymru is seen as the only political party which has taken seriously the interests of Welsh-speakers in their rural northern and western heartlands, the only party whose political philosophy is based on the needs of areas which suffer both from being both economically weak and geographically remote from the London centres of the other political parties.

The centrality of the language to Plaid Cymru is often hidden by today's Party leaders. The party's first pamphlet, *Egwyddorion Cenedlaetholdeb* (Principles of Nationalism), by Saunders Lewis, published in 1926, gave a primacy to the language which has become ever more the unspoken belief of the Gwynedd members who are by now so important to the future of the Party. Lewis wrote that the 'barbarians, the invaders' must be turned into Welsh people, given Welsh thought, Welsh culture and the Welsh language, and Welsh made the only medium of instruction from elementary school to university and the only official language of government. Although the early, furious objections to the use of English anywhere in the Party except in the *Welsh Nationalist* newspaper and in Monmouthshire branches soon vanished, Lewis's views are, as much as ever, the private feelings of most Gwynedd members. The existence of those views is probably the single most important reason for the lop-sided geographical nature of the Party's success.

As in all parties, beliefs are flexible according to the audience; what Lewis wrote is of little consequence to the Valleys, which are concerned about only one sort of barbarians, and they play rugby. Plaid plans to break through in the Valleys by using the same methods which have succeeded successively in Ynys Môn and Ceredigion, and which are now being prepared for use in Carmarthen. A couple of Valley constituencies will be targeted on the basis of past results and present sociological patterns. They will then feel the full blast of the Party's publicity machinery. Opinion polls will be commissioned—perhaps from Party members—and if the results can be made to look favourable, they will be trumpeted month after month from the rooftops.

Plaid is unwilling even to consider that the strategy may not work this time. While political campaigning was important in the Gwynedd and Dyfed victories, more important was a fundamental change in political attitudes locally, a willingness to cast off links with London politics, the willingness to accept a different political philosophy. In Ceredigion, the political change was probably greatest because it was closely allied with Green thinking. Probably the most radical constituency development anywhere in Britain in 1992, Cynog Dafis's victory marked a change as fundamental as that which hit the Valleys in 1922. As in 1922, the Ceredigion result was the fulfilment both of the coming to power of a new generation (a point which applies strongly to all Plaid's General Election victories), and of several years of grass-roots political discussion and policy-making.

Can similar claims honestly be made about Plaid in the Valleys? Adamson has pointed out in works such as *Class, Ideology and the Nation* (1991) that a change is brewing in those Valleys. But has Plaid yet produced the new philosophy that will enable it, rather than the Conservatives, Liberal Democrats or a rejuvenated Labour Party, to take advantage? Plaid has tried any number of philosophies—or perhaps tactics—over the past years. The first was the South-East-based revival under Emrys Roberts in the early-1960s. Gwynfor Evans's stunning by-election victory at Carmarthen in 1966 gave the Party the strength to swing from ruralism to modernism, found a formidable and respected Research Group, and attract research scientist Dr Gareth Morgan Jones to the Party's Cardiff office as Assistant General Secretary. All these combined to produce a Party capable of appealing beyond the literary élite. The disappointments of the 1979 Elections (the Party's advances in Merthyr and the Rhymney Valley were wiped out when the local elections were held on the same day as the General) produced the win-power-through-local-councils idea, and, for a time, the all-conquering policy of 'Democratic Socialism'. Advocacy by Dafydd Elis Thomas, MP for Merionnydd Nant Conwy, helped swing Plaid aboard the hard-Left bandwagon which was at that very time wrecking the Labour Party. Dr (now Lord) Thomas adopted the

44

then-fashionable idea of building a rainbow coalition, including trades unionists, radical Labourites, feminists, anti-nuclear campaigners, liberation theologists, ecologists, anti-racists, and Anglo-Welsh culturalists (with thanks to Dr John Davies, in *The National Question Again* (1985), for the list). To those causes must be added the about-turn on the European Community; once strongly opposed, the Party overnight became enthusiasts because of the prospect of gaining some of the farming vote in the approaching European Parliament Election, although, to be fair, once the electoral imperative vanished the Party remained tied to a European commitment which was not only in line with the party's roots, as defined by Saunders Lewis, but which was also a vote-winner.

The cause of the Left received considerable fillip with the election of Dr Thomas to the Presidency. Yet how deeply held were the Left's views throughout the Party? Although the Hydro Group was never widely popular and never gained many members, its message that the Party's membership was basically traditionalist seemed confirmed when, with the departure of Dr Thomas from the presidency, the Party quickly either downgraded or even forgot its supposed allegiance to Socialism. Plaid easily swung back to its more traditionalist, middle-of-the-road line, even if, for the sake of Party peace, attempts to delete the words from the Constitution were not pressed and the Party under Dafydd Wigley remained theoretically Socialist. At the 1988 Conference, the Party was only two votes short of dropping 'Socialism' from its aims altogether.

Dr Thomas's failure to break into the Valleys was not for lack of trying. During his Presidency, the political and industrial circumstances seemed favourable; the miners' strike was ready-made for Dr Thomas's brand of politics. His vigorous support of the miners, in both word and deed, convinced many who failed to look closely into the Party's Socialist credentials. A small band of Plaid people, plus a group from *Cymdeithas yr Iaith Gymraeg*, went far in forging links with Left-Labour (of some, but not all, varieties) and with the unions, in the hope that they could swing them Plaid-wards. Very few swung, apart from some in the remaining mining fragments of Carmarthenshire where Plaid was already strong. Although the moves failed to add to membership statistics held by Gwerfyl Arthur, Plaid's Administrative Secretary recently made redundant, they had another effect: the Socialist-Nationalists succeeded in convincing many on the Left of the acceptability of Welsh Nationalism; it is difficult to imagine now any repeat of the crude anti-Nationalist propaganda of the 1979 Referendum campaign.

Perhaps the attempted link-up failed because it was trying to join with left-wing Socialism. Significantly, Dr Thomas was friendly with Tony Benn. At the time, Bennism was a power within Labour, pursuing similar policies to those of Thomas in Wales. As I write, Benn is almost a comic figure, no more than tolerated in a Party which blames him for the Election defeats of 1983, 1987, and perhaps 1992. Dr Thomas hooked himself, although it did not seem so at the time, to a dying star. Indeed, to a dying creed, and to a dying way of industrial life. Even during their strike which so shook Britain, far-sighted miners realized there was no long-term future for their industry. Margaret Thatcher's necessary rebuilding of Britain—needlessly bloody as it sometimes was—has ensured that her new industries lack both smoke-stacks and their associated unions and politics. Plaid's democratic Socialism tried to link with a past which was about to vanish.

Plaid liked to believe that the Party's successes in the Valleys were a reflection of its Socialist credentials, when they were far more likely a reflection of opposition politics to Labour. Unlike in South-East England, the Valleys have never been coy about voting one way (for Labour) at a General Election, and another way during the council polls. With Labour so dominant on both the Parliamentary and council scenes, opposition to the alleged arrogance and incompetence of a council's ruling Labour group usually tried to take a 'non-political' form, initially through Ratepayers' groups which, before council reorganization in 1974, gained representation on a variety of Valleys authorities. In Ebbw Vale, they came close to taking control of the Urban District Council. In next-door Nantyglo and Blaina, the local Ratepayers gained much prominence, while proclaiming themselves independent of their neighbours. Throughout the Valleys there has existed a distinctive political culture of opposition; at times this opposition has led to the incumbent Labour Party seeming to be deceptively weak, and Plaid Cymru's leaders seem to be the latest group beguiled by these appearances.

46

Ebbw Vale was once the centre of a hot-bed of opposition groups to Labour; at one time, some local people even wondered whether the seat of MP Michael Foot was safe. But, as is now clear, these were temporary phenomena. In the other direction to Nantyglo and Blaina, at Tredegar, existed yet another opposition group; the difference from its neighbours was only slight, as both personnel and policies seemed similar. The man in Tredegar was hotelier and publican Angus Donaldson, and his Party was the Liberals, although when he moved to become a Liberal councillor in Bedwas, it emerged he was not a member of the Party. Neither were, in fact, the 'Liberal' councillors in Pontypridd. In a Party as weak as were the Liberals locally, Party HQs in Cardiff and London were hardly likely to disown active local councillors using the Party's name. In the three north Gwent towns, the opposition had grown from the grass-roots on claims that the Labour Party locally was out of touch and incompetent. Similar claims fuelled the Ratepayers on Caerffili Urban District Council. In Aberdare, the opposition label was Protectionist, because they were 'protecting' the town from certain plans of the Labour Council.

The Ratepayers' greatest success was in what became West Glamorgan, where a Labour scandal saw them taking power at Swansea's Guildhall, before they were turfed out when they were found to be no better than the previous incumbents. The neighbouring towns of Neath and Port Talbot also gained significant Ratepayer representations. Yet it was precisely because each Ratepayer group was non-political and independent from its neighours—although they all seemed to possess similar policies for 'good government' and cutting down on council spending and services, policies not unlike those now being pursued by Plaid Cymru on Taff-Ely Borough Council—that they lacked staying power. When the strength of the initial local protest eruption had died away, only a few individuals were left to sustain the group. The attraction of extra members and replacement of the leadership proved difficult; sometimes, perhaps, the leaders were individualistic characters who regarded themselves as too indispensable to be replaced, or even argued against.

It has only been those political parties possessing a full, hierarchical branch structure which have managed to find the staying power to present a challenge for Labour to fear. In the industrial South, Labour has seldom had to face such a challenge. The only councils possessing opposition groups of sufficient age, strength and structure are Rhymney Valley (Plaid), Ogwr (Conservatives), Taff-Ely (a Plaid-led Coalition), Islwyn (Plaid), Cynon Valley (Plaid) and Swansea (Conservatives and Liberal Democrats). I exclude South Glamorgan and Monmouth where substantial middle-class areas produce a British-style political pattern. Three of those areas— Caerffili, Bridgend and Taff-Ely—are similar in that they represent valley-mouth communities with substantial immigrant populations (from Cardiff and the upper-valleys), plus middle-class and New Working Class elements. These are areas which would not be out of place in the South East of England. But only in Bridgend is the political development similar to the South East.

Bridgend is the only district where the Conservatives have managed to make headway, coming at one stage within challenging distance of taking control of Ogwr Council. Elsewhere in the Valleys, political activity by Tories between general elections is almost unknown; in Caerffili, for instance, the Party possesses a considerable number of members, but attempts by Party officials to ginger them into life have proved to be in vain, individuals having preferred in the past to stand for election as Independents. A Tory by-election win in early-1993 for a seat on Caerffili Town Council is probably no more than the exception that proves the rule: a newly-formed Young Conservative branch took matters into its own hands and breached local tradition. Whether a group of no more than a dozen youngsters in their twenties will be able to have much effect on the local Tory culture only time will tell.

The difference in Bridgend may be due to the presence of the town of Porthcawl, with its middle-class commuting estates which provide a secure basis for a Conservative Party. From there, the Tories have expanded towards the heart of the borough at Bridgend, aided by the long-serving and able councillor Peter Hubbard-Miles, and David Unwin, an Englishman who pronounced himself—unlike some of his Welsh colleagues—undaunted by the serried ranks of Labour opponents. Unwin also broke tradition by running for some years a Conservative Advice Centre in Bridgend which could have been the model for a Liberal Democrat operation.

Yet the Conservatives have always faced opposition in Ogwr from alternative anti-Labour groups. For many years there existed in the area an active and respected presence from both the Liberals and Plaid Cymru, in the persons of Jennie Gibbs and Ted Merriman. Yet, although both were long-serving councillors, and received much publicity, they both failed to build around themselves a system of branches to extend and preserve their parties' presence. To this day, Ogmore constituency is one of the worst for the Liberal Democrats in a region where they are weak anyway. A similar sort of character is Glyn James, in Rhondda Fach; after Plaid's by-election council wins following the 1992 General Election, one of the Rhondda party's first jobs was to extend rapidly their minimal spread of branches locally, including establishing one in Rhondda Fach!

Opposition political parties in the Valleys pass through several stages of life. The first stage consists of an outstanding local character winning a seat in his or her own ward. If a Party branch is established, it may consist of only family members: the personal eccentricities which enable elections to be won in such areas may militate against working harmoniously with others. Sometimes those eccentricities may militate against everything: a former senior Labour official tells joyously of beating his Plaid opponent by one of the biggest straight-fight majorities in Britain (usually, enough local voters are sufficiently disenchanted with a long-serving councillor to ensure the vote of any solo opponent will rise well above the ridiculous); to make matters worse, the local Plaid branch consisted of hardly anyone apart from the candidate's family.

Yet this personality factor can work in the other direction. Peter Leyshon shocked the Labour Party rigid—or, rather, Labour said he did—when he won a council seat in their Rhondda fortress against an unpopular Labour candidate. This was yet another of those Valley constituencies where the Conservative Party was invisible between General Elections. Leyshon possessed several of the attributes for a successful candidate: he was locally-born, hard-working and popular. He had shown ample proof of these attributes over several years, according to Rhondda Labour stalwarts, through working within their own Party. He had resigned suddenly, expressing in a letter to leader Harold Wilson his opposition to the Party's left-wing stance and attitude to the Common Market. He then turned up in the Conservative Party, both founding and chairing the constituency committee. Leyshon was defeated after one term, and the Party seems to have done nothing locally since.

Perhaps the Tories' time in the Rhondda has come and gone; perhaps the opposition territory and fund of man-power is not great enough for two parties to share, and Plaid has now taken charge locally of the baton of opposition, although the strength of the Plaid challenge can be doubted, despite several by-election wins in the wake of Labour's 1992 General Election disaster. The Nationalists allowed several Labour councillors to be returned unopposed in 1993.

Indeed, the 1993 county contests found no Plaid contestant in a large number of industrial seats. Very seldom was that due to a deal with another non-Labour candidate (a Llanelli area deal is denied by Plaid Cymru). More frequently, Plaid's failure seemed due to the laziness or low quality of that party's local membership, or to their sheer lack of numbers.

In Caerffili, however, where there is a far wider sociological base for an alternative party to Labour, Plaid, by getting in first, seemed to have seized the field, leaving apparently no room for anyone else; Plaid is the only opposition Party actively fighting council elections, with the Tories a force still having to show a willingness to be tested on a scale wider than a single community council by-election, plus two county divisions in 1993, and the Liberal Democrats having to rely on contact telephone numbers.

Despite its failings, Plaid is the only opposition party making any show at a widespread assault on the Valleys. The Nationalists can point to councillors on nine of the twelve Valley councils (and in 24 of the 37 districts throughout Wales). The figures look impressive, until examination reveals that on 18 of these authorities no more than the fingers of one hand are needed to total Plaid's representation. The only decently-sized groups are in Ynys Môn, Meirionnydd and Arfon in the Welsh-speaking North, and in Cynon Valley, Taff-Ely and Rhymney Valley in the South. The three southern groups are well established. The latest district elections presented a mixed message, with substantial gains on those three southern councils countered by equally-substantial losses in Islwyn. The county polls saw good growth in Cynon Valley and Taff-Ely, not much in Rhymney Valley, and continuing slippage in Islwyn.

To what extent is Plaid winning those elections on national Party policy rather than on local grumbles? Asked for Party policies in Taff-Ely contests, they were given, in order, as slamming Labour (said to be by far the most important), local issues, and saving money ('because that was what was needed in the borough'). This is, surely, not a Nationalist, but a Localist, policy, indeed almost a Ratepayer one.

Just to remind voters that they are voting for Plaid Cymru, rather than Plaid Taf-Elai, manifestos also mention Ruling Ourselves (to remind voters they are supporting a Nationalist Party), and the Welsh language. To so many Plaid leaders, the language question is crucial and offers the path to power; ask about national policies, and they so often do not get far beyond the language question. Sending children to Welsh school—the percentage in Caerffili area is now well over 25—is seen as an indication that their parents may be open to voting Plaid, although I doubt if that applies to the young girl in Ysgol Gymraeg Caerffili whose father is Ron Davies, the local Labour MP. To what extent will Welsh-school parents and their children—when they get the vote, as many of them have—be impressed with Plaid council election leaflets carrying scarcely a word of Welsh? And what has the Party to offer the Valleys as a whole, apart from Localism? What signs are there of the Party breaking through to become the Voice of the Community, as Labour has been for so long? Twice Plaid has, indeed, managed that break-through, in Merthyr and Rhymney Valley in 1976, and spectacular indeed was the Merthyr victory, which almost wiped out Labour on that council.

Unfortunately, come the 1979 General Election, the shallowness of that victory was revealed, and it was Plaid's turn to be almost wiped out in Merthyr. Those 1976 votes were proved to have been only lent by voters desperate to protest at the actions of their own Labour Government. While it is fair to protest at the effect of combining local and general elections in districts where voters are habitually willing to vote different ways at each event, the cries of 'foul' from Plaid would have more weight if the Party could point to the existence, somewhere in Merthyr, of a residual strength which would make a showing at the following local election. Of course, there was nothing worth talking of—the Party currently holds only one borough council seat. The situation is healthier in the Rhymney Valley, where the Party 'enjoyed' minority control for three years after winning seats as far north as Bargoed. The Party is still a force to be reckoned with, but only at the bottom of the valley, in and around the Caerffili Basin, where the middle-classes provide a secure voting base in the absence of Conservative and Liberal Democrat candidates. Thoughts of again taking power can be little more than pipe-dreams, when Labour holds 27 seats on the district council, to Plaid's 13, plus six miscellaneous councillors. How can Plaid hope to win in the Valleys when they habitually leave so many seats uncontested, including, for instance, that of Mid Glamorgan's Labour leader, Terry Mahoney, who spent his unexpected spare time boosting the Labour campaign in divisions where there was a Plaid challenge.

Plaid leaders sometimes talk in identical terms to their Liberal Democrat equivalents, as if all that is needed to succeed is a few good people in each town plus a lot of leaflets at the right time. Some of those good people may be Tories, admit Plaid; after all, the 'stand on our own feet and do it ourselves' message is common to both parties.

How much of a realization is there that far more is needed? The party's *Economic Plan for Wales* of 1970 (updated 1977) involved a massive amount of work, and ensured the Party stayed on the political map. Plaid's discussion document *A New Deal for the Valleys* (January, 1993) is a start, and more than the other two opposition parties have done, but is not the equivalent of the 1970 *Plan* which is needed if the Party is to win ground beyond the protest-vote and anti-Labour syndromes. Plaid hope that superior organization will pull them through; Labour blame their Rhondda Borough Council and other seat losses to Plaid during 1992 on their own workers being disheartened after the General Election defeat. If the Labour Party really is beginning to fall apart in the Valleys, the first signs should have appeared during the 1993 county elections. These were the elections no-one wanted except the Home Office. Plaid were hoping to spring a shock in that their members' enthusiasm, even in elections for dying local authorities, was to be pitted against the supposed apathy of a Labour Party whose members saw little point in a poll giving councillors only a two-year term, instead of the usual four. But Plaid's shock-troops never delivered.

Plaid often talks as if there is no essential difference between Gwynedd and Mid Glamorgan. Indeed, in terms of Welsh-born population, Mid Glamorgan is far more Welsh. But there is all the difference in the world between a Welsh-speaking area, remote from metropolitan life, where Plaid can realistically pose as the sole saviour, and English-speaking industrial Valleys where the Labour Party is still entrenched and seems likely to remain so until the Party has been visibly denied all hope of winning entry to Number 10. Plaid seems to lack the confidence that it possesses a new-enough message to sweep out the Labour incumbents. The talk is rather of Labour collapsing internally of its own accord, and of voters drifting away as they gradually realise that Labour will never again form another Government. Plaid's pace of advance in the Valleys is rather like that at General Elections in Wales generally, and has attracted the jibe from the far-left magazine *Y Faner Goch* that Dafydd Williams, Plaid's General Secretary, is planning to host a grand party in 2067, for that will be the year when, on the basis of gaining one single Parliamentary seat at each successive General Election, the Party will have won just over half the Parliamentary seats and can justifiably call for independence at once.

Plaid hopes to emulate Labour's take-over of the Valleys in the 1920s. While Nationalists would like to compare Labour with the Liberals in terms of decay, have they the right to compare themselves politically with Labour, whose votes often doubled or trebled between 1918 and 1922 on the back of the wave of militancy and Marxism which swept the coalfield as a result of the class bitterness and strikes following the war? Where is Plaid's Minority Movement? Where the equivalent of the youngsters trained by the Central Labour College? If any such college exists, it is in the rural areas and it is called *Cymdeithas Cyfamod y Cymry Rhydd*, the Covenanters.

If Plaid is engaged in any realignment, it involves the Greens; the rainbow creed of Dafydd Elis Thomas—although the work of Prof. Phil Williams on the ground in the constituency must not be under-emphasized—helped create the alliance with the Greens which was the single most important factor handing Ceredigion and Pembroke North to Cynog Dafis. While the by-Election feel created by enthusiastic Plaid workers, and the age of the Liberal Democrat candidate and state of that Party's organization were important, it was the Green link which gave Dafis the third-highest swing of the General Election (he was beaten by Govan and Ribble Valley, where by-elections had intervened). It gave him a new political philosophy —'we must live within the planet's ability to absorb the effects of our actions'—which struck home with rural voters. And it gave Plaid credibility in terms of votes: combining the support from two traditions dramatically widened the Plaid appeal to immigrants and effectively killed the wasted-votes argument.

Yet this particular alliance could not be repeated anywhere else in Wales, apart from in the silly-votes region of Gwent. Had it been possible in Carmarthen—and had electors believed Plaid candidate Rhodri Glyn Thomas was as green as Dafis—the success would have been the same, as Conservative voters flocked to Plaid to rid themselves of tbe Labour Party. Despite the committed work of Green Euro-candidate Brig Oubridge, it proved impossible. The Greens are, in fact, deeply split over working with Plaid, far more so than are the Nationalists, although there have been Plaid rumblings from Gwynedd. It is not only the 'nitrogenous green fields' which Ceredigion Labour candidate John Davies expects to see on the farms of Plaid supporters which is annoying some of the Greens. A few (or perhaps more) of the Greens are colonially-minded English who dislike the Welsh, in particular their language which they believe, probably sometimes correctly, is being used as a barrier against them. More, however, take the old Socialist and inter-nationalist line, that all nationalism is bad, that it is nationalism which causes wars, and so on.

There is now no doubt that the post-imperial troubles of eastern Europe are capable of harming Plaid's advance. The heady days of the New World Order have collapsed amidst the civil wars of the Balkans. The peace dividend, so beloved of Plaid's now-declining pacifist wing, is vanishing as the call goes out for a larger army—with lots of infantrymen—to help keep the peace throughout the world. A Welsh Nationalist who was about to rush off to newly-free Lithuania had to be reminded that it was worth examining how they treated their linguistic minorities, in particular the Polish-speakers who form a majority in the capital Vilnius, a city which had been seized by the Poles in 1920 and not returned until 1939. A prominent Welsh-speaking Nationalist, bemoaning the state of Eastern Europe, said it made her question her support for Plaid. Once, it was the example of third-world indpendence movements which sparked support for Plaid. Now, the world is changing, and even a writer in *The Observer* (10 January 1993) can support French ideas for a right of international armed intervention that looks not unlike some varieties of nineteenth-century imperialism. With international co-operation now the watchword, it is perhaps fortunate for Plaid that the Party has since its earliest days emphasized that it is not independence that is being demanded, but freedom, self-government, subordination to an international authority, and a seat in the League of, and now United, Nations.

The Party's greatest weakness is its lack of strength outside the *Fro Gymraeg*. Of 200 Welsh branches prior to the 1992 Election, 65 were in Plaid-held seats in Gwynedd. When Ceredigion and Pembroke North and Carmarthen are added, the total reaches 99. Outside this area, the only constituency which can boast even 10 branches is Caerffili; then comes Pontypridd with six. There are more branches in Anglesey and Arfon (46) than in all of the industrial Valleys (44). And, comparing with figures given by Alan Butt Philip in *The Welsh Question* (1975), the imbalance towards Welsh-speaking areas is worsening by the year. Were detailed membership figures known, the position would probably be seen to be worse because, while Gwynedd branches are large, many others are small.

Distribution of Plaid Branches

	1938	1965-9	% branches	% pop'n	1992	% branches
North West	45	54	22	8	71	37
North East	22	27	12	13	15	8
Powys	2	18	6	4	11	6
West	16	57	24	12	42	22
Glamorgan	18	66	27	46	51	26
Gwent	1	19	9	17	4	2
Totals	104	241			194	

Another Plaid weakness has been that it has been overwhelmingly a middle-class Party (in a nation which Party leaders liked to say was classless). The survey by Butt Philip found (before it was halted by Party officials) that half of activists represented the 'knowledge industry'. The make-up is unlikely to have changed much in twenty years. While once a weakness, this may become a strength with the growth of the new working-class which considers itself middle-class, with increasing emphasis by the growing proportion of 'haves' within Welsh society on cultural factors and ethnicity—hence the increased interest in the Welsh language and the burgeoning growth in Welsh-medium schools. Colin Williams, in *National Separatism,* adds to this the Plaid argument that the forces of modernization and centralization combine to produce an urge for political fragmentation. In other words, as the world gets more complicated, with institutions controlled from ever more remote locations, the desire increases for the local or regional level to be given the maximum control possible.

Plaid was launched in 1925 with a policy which seemed to look back more to the Middle Ages than to the future: 'The principles of our nationalism mean going back to the principles of the Middle Ages,' wrote Saunders Lewis in *Egwyddorion Cenedlaetholdeb.* Nationalists do, on occasion, dream of those days when Wales was free, although when Jan Morris put such dreams of a rural utopia on paper (in *The Independent,* 1 August 1992) she was compared by angry correspondents with Serb and Croat dreamers in pre-ethnic cleansing days! Plaid once contained within its ranks dreamers and extremists of several colours who could be guaranteed to increase the President's blood pressure and provide a good headline. Most, but not all have gone, pushed out by the grey technocrats now in control, the people who reckon an annual conference is a television show, rather than a forum to debate and decide policy. It is, however, the Party's strength that people who were once capable of holding electoral fortune as their hostage have largely vanished. It enables a clearer split to be demonstrated between Plaid and the less-constitutionalist Nationalist movements, *Cymdeithas yr Iaith,* the *Cyfamodwyr,* and the multiplicity of individuals and tiny groups who make and have made up *Meibion Glyndwr.*

The technocrats are more likely than the dreamers to work to make use of the System at the same time as they try to change or abolish it. The archetypal technocrat is a Cardiff middle-class

Welsh-speaker, the sort of person much reviled by language fundamentalists for arguing that even a weak Welsh Language Act would contain enough strengths to enable the Welsh Language Board to work a considerable and, in some cases, fundamental change in the position of the language, particularly in the Welsh-speaking Wales whose continuing existence is crucial if the language is to possess a long-term future.

To revile quangos as undemocratic involves a failure to understand that they are largely administrative machines carrying out tasks which many good democrats would say should never be the concern of elected members; to argue that they are unaccountable ignores the quangos' accountability to the Secretary of State and to the Parliament which Wales voted to maintain by a 4-1 majority in the 1979 Referendum. Yet it is the increasing Welsh accent of the governmental system which is currently Nationalism's greatest growth sector. The contested decision—which could yet be reversed—to lump Wales with England in the new environmental agency, while Scotland is given its freedom, is notable as being one of the few times that the Conservative Government has failed to establish a Wales-only body. Labour claims that most of these new quangos' chairmen, when they can be politically identified, are Tories, obscures the fact that at least two high-profile bosses support Plaid, and a good few in England are Labour.

Very occasionally can be heard within Plaid the argument that more can be gained quickly through administrative means and quango-memberships than through conventional politics. Did, for instance, the introduction of compulsory teaching of the Welsh language have to await a Language Act and combatative political argument, or was it a decision by administrative fiat, the result of politicking by middle-class experts who created a new political agenda by working from the grass-roots upwards, and then won by force of argument the support of the middle-classes who also run the civil service, local government and the quangos?

Perhaps we are moving away from the day of the Common Man, and entering that of the Intelligent Man, who is a little grey, like Premier Major, but who is ultimately fair-minded, and is willing to be convinced by a well-presented argument in favour of a line of advance which remains within the Grey Man's rules and does not attempt a revolution, except by gradual steps. Intelligent Man often has a low regard for party politics, seeing it as too confrontational and too unwilling to accept that the political opposition possesses some good ideas which deserve adapting, rather than rejecting with a knee-jerk. Perhaps Intelligent Quango Man will be the political power of the future, and the political parties most willing to accept his existence will best be able to set the political agenda of the future.

As the section of the United Kingdom which gives the highest voting support to Labour, Wales will be most affected by any decline affecting that Party. The Socialists have, of course, already been evicted from Parliamentary seats in most of Wales, by a variety of Nationalists, Conservatives and Liberals. It is hard to believe though, surveying the Valleys, that the Party will ever lose hold on its remaining Welsh stronghold, although no doubt the same was said about the Liberals 70 years ago. It was a generation change which saw off Lloyd George's Party; perhaps the class change as epitomised by the emergence of Adamson's New Working Class will be the impetus needed for a repeat performance.

Which Party will take over in the Valleys is still not totally clear, although Plaid would disagree. A revived Labour Party in the form of the SDP would have been the best bet; but that Party is now gone, and the Liberal Democrats are almost totally absent from the region. Their history (even though we are talking of events 70 years ago), plus their lack of effort ever since, seems to preclude the Conservatives. This leaves Plaid Cymru, which is the only Party with widespread representation in the Valleys. Yet the Valleys' attitude to Plaid Cymru is ambivalent: advances in one town are partly counter-balanced by retreats elsewhere. At present, Plaid so often seems to lack a clear social message which the Valleys so much need; the Party depends too much on the old Ratepayer battle-cries of Value for Money and reductions in spending. Perhaps Plaid will win through by default, and those much-needed policies will be developed after the Party has taken power.

In Welsh-speaking Wales, the future is clear—unless an individual Plaid MP fails to come up to the mark and is ejected by the Conservatives who are, by now, the only challengers in the *Fro Gymraeg* and increasing in strength. Plaid has already faultlessly managed one generation change—in Meirionnydd Nant Conwy—and it will be some years before the next MP stands down. The next Election should see Carmarthen in the bag, after which they can wait for Denzil Davies to grow old in Llanelli: he was born in 1938, so there's a good few years of life there yet!

If the Liberal Democrats keep to their tentative ideas of concentrating on Anglo-Wales, we may yet see them emulating the successes of their colleagues in South-West England. The Party has little hope of competing successfully against Plaid Cymru; clever targeting of seats could result, though, in the gaining or regaining of Brecon and Radnor and Conwy, plus the retention of Montgomery. National trends—in particular the fate of the Labour Party—will determine what happens to the Liberal Democrat vote along the south and north Wales coastal belts; the job of local Party members is to ensure that a well-honed organization is in place to take advantage. In most places, that task of preparing the organization has hardly begun.

Labour members in Wales find it hard to admit their Party is facing anything but temporary difficulties. The south Wales and Clwyd Parties show, indeed, a healthy ability to rebuild and renew. The Valleys' MPs are producing more quality political material than for some years. Insulated by Offa's Dyke and the Brecon Beacons, it is hard in south Wales to believe the truth of reports about the poor state of the Party elsewhere. A super-human effort by the Party could, indeed, win Labour the next General Election, but it would probably be by a tiny margin, and would be followed by another decade of Tory rule. Failure in 1996 or thereabouts would spell the end of Labour as a national Party; it would revert to what it was in the 1920s, a regional Party, with south Wales as one of its bastions. It is difficult to imagine Plaid over such a short time-scale managing the two-stage trick of taking over the new unitary Councils—particularly, as is possible, the polls are held on the same day as the Euro-election, with high Labour and Tory turnouts swamping a Plaid vote, even if Plaid's support were boosted as in the 1990 Euro-poll—and then translating those victories to the Westminster stage. And if Labour hold on long enough in the Valleys after their destruction nationally, that may give time for either of the other parties to move in as main challengers.

Postscript

The pending disappearance of the eight Welsh counties—and the unseemly rush to ditch Gwent for Monmouthshire—spawned fears that the 1993 elections would prove a flop, with insufficient interest, insufficient candidates and insufficient voters. Although the new councils were due to vanish in only two years, those fears proved to be groundless. In some areas, machine-politics kept the democratic bandwagon rolling; in others, the dream of David vanquishing Goliath ensured the existence of interest, candidates, voters, and lost seats.

The Conservative expected to be hammered, and so it proved. As the table (page 29) shows, their unrelenting decline in the number of seats held has continued. It is now down to less than one-quarter of the percentage achieved in the halcyon days (for the Tories) of the 1976 mid-term county elections of the Harold Wilson Government. Conservative Central Office at Whitchurch, in Cardiff, are, in public, little concerned about this decline. Mid-term blues, they say, only this time it is we who are suffering. But at each 'mid-term', the Tory suffering gets worse. Listening to some Conservatives, it is difficult to avoid the feeling that the party, in truth, is not much interested in local government. So often, the only interest seems to be in how to reduce spending, or how to cut Labour down to size.

From studying election figures showing, for instance, that not a single Tory in South Glamorgan won a plurality of the vote, it would seem that this message may have got through to the electorate. In the party's once-solid districts, voters are flocking in droves to the Liberal Democrats. The average drop in the Tory vote in South Glamorgan in May compared with the previous county elections was 8.6%; the biggest falls, of up to 25%, were in districts where the Liberal Democrats were the challengers.

The continuing decline of the Tory presence in the council chambers of Wales—by now they control only Monmouth, having lost the Vale of Glamorgan—is perhaps a further sign that Labour is continuing to formulate the agenda for local government in Wales. Yet the Tory decline is largely restricted to local authorities. And the belief that the party is being ejected from Cardiff seems poorly founded. The suburban drift which has destroyed so many American cities has still to cross the Atlantic: Conservatives still live in the city in great numbers, but they vote for their own candidates only during Parliamentary contests. If either of the two governing parties is having trouble with its General Election vote in the capital, it is Labour: it is they who usually suffer most at such times from the attentions of the Liberal Democrats and their predecessors.

Yet, although the drop in South Glam's 1993 Tory vote seems to mark the county out as an extension of the great South of England revolt, something different has been happening in Newport. The Tory vote in that town actually rose over 1989, with a two per cent swing from Labour. There was no such good news from the surrounding county, where votes fell, or were static, in every seat where comparison could be made with 1989. Were Newport's results a fluke, or were they an indication of an improving organization, which had been expected to deliver gains at the previous borough council elections? The Tories' total of seats throughout Wales fell by eight to 31.

The Liberal Democrats have never possessed an all-Wales presence. Neither have Plaid Cymru in the council chambers. But at least the Nationalists can point to a couple of ordinary members in every district—even if care has to be taken to shield new-comers from some of the party's more eccentric office-holders. The Lib Dem councillor strength has historically been limited to a few towns; this year's achievement was to add their first industrial town to that list—Llanelli, where votes were taken from Labour.

Elsewhere, the party is embarrassing in its inability to strike at the Labour vote in county elections. With comparisons only generally possible in South Glamorgan, it was in the usually Tory wards that the Liberal Democrats scored. Are these votes on loan solely for the period of Tory protest? And why did the party fail to make England-style advances? In a reflection of what happened in the General Election, a barrier seems to exist for the party at the Severn Bridge, with success in Wales much more elusive than in southern England. Why else did the Liberal Democrat percentage of the vote fall in eight of the 28 contested wards in Cardiff? Throughout Wales, the party gained 12 seats, giving it 34.

If the Liberal Democrats are disappointed in their inability to win a wider breakthrough, how much more must be Labour? Still the giants of the county halls, the party suffered 12 losses (notably around Llanelli), giving it a total of 270 seats. Transport House in Cardiff argues that local factors are to blame. Often they are. But how was it that the party lost votes in nine of 29 seats in Cardiff? The Liberal Democrats also suffered in some wards. But overall the Lib Dems came off better, with a 4.8% increase in their vote, compared with Labour's 3.2%.

In Mid Glamorgan, Labour's record was much worse, with losses in two-thirds of the seats where a comparison could be made with 1989; in Gwent, half of such seats showed a loss of votes. In the Valleys it can be argued that the retreat is the result of the introduction of greater pluralism into local politics.

That it is Plaid Cymru which usually provides that touch of pluralism is causing more worry within Transport House than is admitted. Plaid like to argue that a generational voting shift is taking place, and many in the Labour Party half-fear they are right. Plaid is certainly the only party which so far has managed to sustain a consistent challenge in the Valleys. The lack of a rival means it is impossible to judge accurately whether the shift from Labour is because of opposition to the County Hall incumbents and their policies, or because of a positive preference for Nationalism.

As the General Election results seem to indicate little love for Plaid policies, perhaps Labour should examine its propaganda constantly denigrating the Valleys. To state, as did a senior Valleys Labour figure, that Seville, in Spain, is richer than the Valleys, invites ridicule from European officialdom. To claim that the Valleys' Initiative is largely a myth invites the question as to who they think paid for the wholesale clearance of the remains of the coal industry from the Cynon Valley. Labour propaganda is now so much out of step with the facts that it would be no surprise if the electorate were beginning to vote for any opposition party which appeared. Perhaps people are fed up with listening to gloom and doom from Labour politicians, particularly when it is at odds with what they see with their own eyes and with official figures accepted by everyone else— officials of Labour-controlled local authorities included.

That some of Labour's senior figures realise the party could be facing problems was underlined at the party's Wales conference this year with the launch of Cymru Charter, an examination of what is wrong with the party, and how to rectify it. What a pity that the document was so similar to the analysis published all of six years ago. Behind both was Derek Gregory, the lively leader of UNISON in Wales. After diagnosing at Llandudno this May some of the party's problems—such as lack of youngsters—he and his trade union colleagues then put forward the sort of remedy which many consider a turn-off from the past—closer links with the unions.

The most disappointed party after the county elections of May 1993 must have been Plaid Cymru. Despite increasing its total number of seats by 14 (almost half of the gains being in Gwynedd) to 41, the party fell far short of its expectations. As members struggled to pick themselves up after a disappointing campaign, the party proceeded to tear into itself over the futures of its General Secretary and Administrative Secretary. The Thatcherite way in which their posts have been upended, with both being pushed out of office, augurs badly for the short-term future of the party. Claims by some party activists that the row was responsible for the party's poor election performance are difficult to believe. Yet the issue is a hostage to fortune. The claim to be a socialist party must now be difficult to sustain.

The row raises major questions about the remoteness from ordinary members of the Parliamentary Party. All M.P.s are said to agree on the changes, although the constituency parties of two were vehemently opposed. Spending almost five days a week in London, all MPs grow remote from their constituents. Plaid is now becoming as London-centred as the other British parties; logically, the party's head office should be moved to somewhere such as the Vauxhall Bridge Road. Adding Dafydd Williams to the Parliamentary staff will only increase the amount of power lodged in London, and further side-line the Cardiff 'headquarters'. Truly a strange position for a Nationalist party to be in!

The reasons behind the staffing changes have never been made clear, apart from a general belief that the party could perform better. As indeed, it could. Firstly, local branches could find some election candidates. Forty years ago, the Liberals managed to find candidates to fight every seat in London suburbs, although none of them ever won. Why is Plaid so far from emulating that feat in the industrial areas of Wales where party politics long ago took over in the council chamber?

In Mid Glamorgan, Plaid could have taken control of the Council Chamber only if almost every candidate fielded had won. Yet seats were left uncontested even in Rhondda, where the party had trumpeted in the wake of by-election successes following the General Election that Labour's day was almost over. In some Mid Glamorgan divisions, the party's advance was spectacular, in Aberaman South (where a too-long serving Labour councillor was ejected), Llanharan (with Janet Davies, a senior party official and leader of Taff-Ely Borough Council), Tonteg, and Ystrad. But elsewhere the advance was often painfully slow. Even in Parliamentary seats held by Plaid, the vote sometimes fell.

Plaid had planned that these county elections would be the springboard for the party's sweeping to power when elections for the unitary councils are held next summer. On present showings, that is unlikely to happen anywhere ... unless a host of long-serving Independent councillors retire (Independents hold 122 county council seats, a drop of eight on four years ago) and are replaced by politicised youngsters.

The only politicised area where Plaid has a hope is the proposed Glamorgan Valleys council. An analysis by the party locally shows Plaid's share of the vote at the county contest shot up to 42%. In Taff-Ely and Cynon Valley, that figure is a realistic statement of the party's support at local government elections, as all seats were contested. But no-one could be found to contest four of the 11 in Rhondda, and that was after those by-election wins in 1992.

According to social and political theorists, the Labour Party can be likened to an over-ripe apple whose time has passed. Radice, with his Fabian pamphlet, *Southern Discomfort*, and Adamson, of the University of Glamorgan, are at one in perceiving deep social changes among its erstwhile voters which Labour has not responded to. Adamson points to a change which goes beyond jobs to life-style, and to homes increasingly semi-detached rather than terraced; he points to the willing acceptance by many Labour voters of late twentieth-century adjuncts, such as personal transport (i.e. motor cars), hi-fis, do-it-yourself equipment and solitary sports, such as jogging.

Both Radice and Adamson ask to what extent is Labour adequately appealing to this newly-affluent class. Far too much Labour propaganda seems not to be addressed to this ever-increasing group, but rather to an under-class of long-term unemployed, of single mothers, and of small specialised interest groups. The Party continues to pride itself on its link with trade unions of which fewer and fewer of its voters are members. As the trade union link at voter level withers, the union bosses themselves seem to justify their dinosaur image with their unrelenting battles to maintain their influence at the top of the Party.

Adamson tries to link the development of his New Working Class to Plaid Cymru's advances in the '60s and '70s; unfortunately, he underplays the roles in this of, first, the international youth revolt and reaction against authority and, secondly, the power of the unstable and often unthinking protest vote, which was aimed then against Labour as it is today against John Major's Tories.

Peter Hain's Neath Declaration of 1992 points to similar dangers, to the creation by youngsters of a 'culture quite at odds with that of their parents—one that will inevitably lead to a weakening of the ties of Labourism, if not a complete break, in the absence of a Socialist renewal'. The Declaration warns against south Wales following the example of traditional industrial areas in other parts of the UK 'where Labour support has either been significantly reduced or even marginalised'.

Similarly, Radice points out the dangers to Labour. He writes in his Fabian pamphlet, *Southern Comfort*, about the dire problems facing the people's party in south-east England. Welsh ostriches will dispute the relevance to south Wales, without realising how much our industrial valleys have changed physically over the last decade—never mind mentally—during 14 years of Toryism. In my own Rhymney Valley, middle-class, semi-detached estates, once largely confined to Caerffili and Ystrad Mynach, have now spread up to Penpedairheol (between the massive and gloomy council estate of Hengoed and the run-down industrial town of Bargoed) and to the old working-class village of Nelson. These estates could almost be sited in the south-east of England. Labour might believe these new homes are as safe electorally as are Rhymney Valley strongholds such as Rhymney town; but is it perhaps significant that the Plaid presence, once largely restricted to the Caerffili-Ystrad Mynach belt, is now worming its way into Nelson? The residents of these homes are almost all locals, and formerly solid Labour-voters—but their membership of the New Working Class gives them so many of the attributes which Radice in the South-East found led to refusal to vote Labour—the south-easterners walked into the polling booth in 1992 intending to vote Labour, and walked out again having put their X against the Conservative name.

These new Welsh semi-detached dwellers will follow the South-East of England in no longer considering themselves working-class: in no longer placing emphasis on the (Labour-oriented) community; in pursuing a life-style which is home, family and DIY based; in maintaining only low trade union membership; having worked to improve themselves, they would believe far less in Labour-style equality, preferring Tory-style values; and strongly opposing (as do many continuing Labour voters) that party's perceived preference for helping those among the poor who are 'undeserving'.

Penpedairheol and Nelson are only the forerunners of the advance of this new life-style into the Valleys. The Draft Rhymney Valley District Plan, recently published, proposes significant homes construction in almost every community, including many where new-style private housing is rare and where private developers have previously shown little interest—villages such as Deri, Fochriw, Bargoed, Abertysswg and Rhymney. Even largely council-estate villages such as Bedwas would gain a periphery which could serve as the basis for a political assault on one of Labour's last bastions.

The closeness of the 1992 result in terms of seats conceals the extent to which the bourgeoisification of Labour's vote has proceeded apace. The division line between the old world (of Attlee and a working-class party) and the modernist polling booths of today was probably the Election of 1970, which swept out Wilson and swept in Heath. Never again could Labour gain UK percentages of the vote in the upper-40s. The table on page 13 which reveals how Labour's vote has behaved in Wales is closely replicated in the UK figures of the percentage of voters voting Labour (in brackets are the party's lead over the Tories, with a minus sign indicating a Tory lead):

1945—48.0% (8.4); 1950—46.1% (2.7); 1951—48.8% (0.8); 1955—46.4% (−3.3); 1959—43.8% (−5.6); 1964—44.1% (0.7); 1966—48.0% (6.1); 1970—43.1% (3.3); February 1974—37.2% (−0.7); October 1974—39.2% (3.4); 1979—36.9% (−7.0); 1983—27.6% (−14.8); 1987—30.8% (−11.5); 1992—34.4% (−7.5).

Britain is changing, as is Wales. The fascination of Wales is the entry into the successor-stakes of a third nag, Plaid Cymru. While sensible punters may be more than happy to risk a flutter in England, they would be best advised in Wales to keep their cash in their pockets while the Welsh form remains so unclear.